Oberon Kant's BIG BOOK of WINE

by Oberon Kant, AO, BSE

Foreword by Sir Les Patterson

www.Spittoon.com.au

Hardie Grant Books

First published in 2002
by Hardie Grant Books
12 Claremont Street
South Yarra
Victoria 3141
www.hardiegrant.com.au

This is a work of fiction. Any resemblance to any person, living or dead, is purely coincidental. No animals were harmed during the writing of this book. Do not read this book under the influence of alcohol.

Where applicable, every effort has been made to trace copyright holders of the photographs. In most instances photographs used are out of copyright. The publisher regrets any errors or omissions, and would like to hear from anyone who has information otherwise.

National Library of Australia Cataloguing-in-Publication Data:

Kant, Oberon.
Oberon Kant's big book of wine.

ISBN 1 74064 068 3.
1. Wine and winemaking. 2. Wine and winemaking – Humor

641.872

Edited by Dale Campisi
Design and typesetting by Phil Campbell
Printed in Australia by the Australian Book Connection.

Photo credits:
Page 4: Steven Siewert/Courtesy of *The Age*.
Pages 79, 82, 85, 94, 102, 132, 134, 147, 149: Barry Schitthe.

Valediction

Out of the crooked timber of humanity nothing straight was ever made.

Immanuel Kant – my great ancestor (and probably the greatest Kant of them all)

Dedication

This book is dedicated to my great mate Nelson Mandela, whom I bonded with over a case of KWV Pinotage during vintage on Robben Island.

Devotion

There is a lot of cant talked about wine, yet even cant is better than total ignorance and too much respect better than none at all. Would we want to see all courtesy, all charm, all grace banished from the world? Then wine would go with them.

Baron Philippe de Rothschild, in his autobiography, *Milady Vine*, written by Joan Littlewood

Foreword

This is a book I should've written myself since I have been dabbling in the finer things of life for a lot longer than Oberon Kant.

When I was knee-high to a grasshopper, wine was something derros drank under bridges. There were also places down the wrong end of Pitt Street in Sydney and Flinders Street in Melbourne where the muscatel sippers used to congregate. It was a pathetic sight seeing those poor bastards staggering out with their bottles of tawny Port and Royal Purple Para while real Australians got full on beer. There was a big change in the fifties when the Dago fraternity introduced espresso machines, cappuccinos and spaghetti that didn't come out of a tin. Our world was turned upside down as the wine saloons closed down and reopened, as bistros where piss elegant Australians who had just bought their first wooden Fler salad bowl and maybe scored one overseas trip sat around in their suede desert boots, smoking Rothmans and getting quietly schickered on Coonawarra Claret. Then came the age of the Carlton townhouse and the Paddo terrace, the ad man and the brown and orange macramé wall hanging. By then, trendy Australians were actually collecting wine. That's to say, they'd buy it and not drink it all that night.

Barossa Pearl stopped being the housewife's tipple. Women who needed a drink before breakfast – and there were plenty of them, God love 'em – could attack the cardboard wine cask in the fridge, and there was no way their suspicious hubbies or handicapped children could check the rapidly diminishing booze level in one of them casks.

But now Australian oeneology has come of age. My mate Oberon wrote the book, and this is the book. I've sipped vino with Bronny all over the planet and at 35,000 feet on Air Paraguay there's nothing like a nice oakey Oz Chardonnay and an obliging Latino hostie to help you forget the turbulance.

Bronny is old-fashioned and cutting-edge at the same time. He always wears a nice tie and if he hasn't got the Order of Australia then there's something radically wrong with this fantastic country of ours where every used-car salesman and every shonky polly has got one of them blue and gold buttons on his hand-stitched Hong Kong lapel. You can chuck all those other wine books into your marble pedal-bin. This informative volume is all you need when you've made the sophisticated decision to go for the grape.

Bottoms up!

LES PATTERSON

Oberon Kant's
Big Book of Wine

by Oberon Kant, AO, BSE

Contents

Wine lovers everywhere celebrate the publication of this book.

Introduction

Breeding, humility, what school you attended, and where your mother shops are crucial in the appreciation of Fine Wine. A donkey cannot win the Kentucky Derby; self-importance may maketh the advertising man, but not the gentleman; autodidacticism is an outrage; and only a brute would let his mother shop anywhere.

These are the strictures by which I have lived my life since birth – indeed, since conception. Without these tenets to guide me I should never have gained my unrivalled and imperious mastery of wine. And yet this also saddens me, for I fear I am the last of the Mohicans. As Western Civilisation falls further into decline and the last rays of a once glorious empire's sun fade into a never-ending night, the social cancer that is moral laxity will prevent any of us from achieving what I have achieved. More importantly, it prevents anyone achieving my achievements in the manner in which I achieved them.

Thusly I have set out to lay down, in one volume, THE TRUTH ABOUT WINE. Yet I have not gone willingly. My publisher, agent, immediate family, and friends in government have repeatedly pleaded with me to reacquaint the world with the lore of wine. Like Cincinnatus before me, I have left my meadow and plough to save Rome – although in my case, I have reluctantly come out of retirement to inject some intellectual rigour into the field of what now passes for wine literature. The simile is therefore not as strong as it could be. Cincinnatus was only saving Rome from the Aequians; I am fighting for the survival of civilisation itself.

But perhaps some of my younger readers would now like to learn first hand, in my own words, my own personal story.

My mother was a Mitford sister – I can't quite recall which one. My father, Cnut Kant, was Mayor of Oslo, a fashion designer and mentor to Le Corbusier. I was born mid-air while in a flying boat from Lahore, India to Hyde Park, London. In those days, flying boats serviced the then nascent take-away curry industry. My early tastes were largely influenced by my wet nurse, who previously worked with the Churchill family. I was educated thoroughly by Rudolf Steiner at home.

During a childhood holiday to my uncle Baron Von Überkant's *schloss* in Barbados, I fell into an open cask of 1796 Malmsey – the finest Madeira ever made. It was an experience that was to change my life forever.

After a lengthy recuperation in Mexico City I realised I was a child prodigy. I awarded myself the very first Master of Wine qualification and fundamentally changed forever the way quality people experience Fine Wine. I was the first to ever LISTEN to wine. The bottle was a 1900 Mouton Rothschild *en magnum*. I was drinking it at breakfast while staying with my mentor and father figure, Baron Philippe de Rothschild, one bank holiday. The fact I could hear the wine speak surprised me not; what it said *was* startling, however, and became permanently etched on my mind. It was something along the lines of '*Second je suis, premier je serais. Mouton ne charge.*' For those without the requisite French tutelage, this roughly translates as 'Second I am, first I will be. This one's on the house.'

Now, many rich and fruitful years later, I have taken time out from a life that is an endless round of lucrative celebrity speaking engagements to prepare this weighty tome – my very own pièce de résistance. This work not only silences my vociferous editors, but also acts as a last-ditch attempt to rescue wine from the clammy, licentious hands of popular culture; the ignoble excesses of modern lifestyle journalism; and the misshapen, drooling lips of the lumpen proletariat.

Cheers!

OBERON KANT, AO, BSE
WANGILLIALLIGONG-ON-MURRAY, SOUTH AUSTRALIA

How to use this book

The intricate symbols, scores, cross-referencing, footnotes, rambling anecdotes and digressions explained in full.

Affix stamp here.
Anon

There are two ways to use this book: the right way and the wrong way. Readers with a pre-1960s education will stand a better chance than the youngsters; both will be greatly advantaged by following these simple steps:

Read the book from cover to cover in one sitting, preferably in a reading room of one of the world's great libraries.

Take extensive notes. If the book belongs to you, feel free to annotate the margins IN PENCIL ONLY.

Write a short letter to me care of my publisher; state succinctly how my book has ameliorated your understanding of wine and, indeed, of life.

Memorise what you consider to be a half-dozen or so key sentences from different sections of the book and sprinkle these quotations liberally in your daily conversation. For instance, if your secretary mentions she is having some difficulty with her mother's second husband, reply: 'Well, Miss Mousetrap, as Oberon Kant so eloquently puts it in his *Big Book of Wine* … ' and then insert the relevant quote. Of course, if you know me personally, you may care to say: 'As my great mate Oberon Kant puts it … '.

Key to symbols

🍷 whenever this symbol appears you should order a glass of red house wine, if you are not already drinking one.

this indicates it is time to put some more white wine in the refrigerator.

not a symbol, but a decorative motif that adds some charm and Watteau-like romantic beauty to my book.

The star system employed herein

☠ Not very good.

☠☠ Still not very good.

☠☠☠ Wine suitable for novices or 'occasional' drinkers.

☠☠☠☠ An overpriced wine.

🏆🏆🏆🏆🏆: The wines I drink or those served to me by friends.

⚓⚓⚓⚓⚓⚓: Madeira.

The 100-point system employed herein

Fifty is equivalent to zero where 89.5 equals 16 and 100 is perfection. Most wines sit between 80 and 92.5; hence this is really the 12.5 system. One hundred of anything always reminds me of decimalisation. I abhor decimalisation.

Vintage years

References to vintages will appear in the following format:

86: wine from 1986.

86: wines from 1986 that I don't like.

86: wines from 1986 that no one likes.

86: wines from 1986 that are quite good. If you happen to find yourself reading this book upside down, this underlined reference will help you differentiate 86 from 98.

'86: an error.

(Not to be confused with 86, which indicates a score. See above.)

Medals and trophies

Medals and such have always been popular in the wine game. We English like them as they remind us of our past military valour; the French like them as they suggest a history of military valour that is, of course, non-existent; and the Australians like them as they remind that strange race of the Olympic Games. The people of North America also like medals as they help to sell things.

There is much confusion about medals and what they actually mean. The following is correct procedure, as used in this guide:

Gold: of acceptable commercial standard; a vulgar wine with no subtlety.

Silver: probably a very good wine; Fine to Very Fine.

Bronze: a wine one can drink without much effort.

Copper: a medal presented to red wine which is in need of 'finishing'. This medal is usually very small, in order that it might be dropped in the neck of the bottle.

Iron: a medal awarded to young, tannic Cabernet Sauvignon.

Lead: a rather heavy medal.

Tin: a medal presented to children who like to play winemaker.

The Kant system

A wine merit ranking system based on the enthusiastic use of superlatives.

Good: a good wine.

Fine: a Fine Wine.

Very fine: a very Fine Wine.

Very fine indeed: I like this.

Outstanding: of a quality normally only associated with the wines served to me by friends or in the first-class section of my airline of choice, Air Paraguay, to which I consult.

(NB: Madeira is without doubt the best-suited high-altitude wine. When flying Air Paraguay, ask for Special Reserve Verdelho in first class and the Reserve Bual when relaxing on the open-air smoking deck located just behind the cockpit.)

Chapter 1

The marvellous story of wine

My own very intimate history of the role my many ancestors and I have played in the development of wine – culminating in this, its Golden Age.

Red red wine goes to my head; makes me forget that I still need you so; memories don't go.
My great mate Edward de Bono

Since ancient times, when man first held aloft a rough-hewn drinking vessel to his primitive, hairy gods, wine has been the lifeblood of every human civilisation ever to have walked or crawled across the face of the earth. Wine is the very conduit through which man has chosen to distil his experiences; his history; his laughter; his tears; his science; his artistry; his craftsmanship; his poetry; his seduction; his laughter and his tears over the millennia. At every unexpected turn, every sharp hairpin corner and every cruel, bitter twist of fate that destiny has chosen to hurl in man's path, wine has emerged from the shadows to soothe, console, redeem and placate. Wine is all this and much, much more.

Despite the many Golden Ages of Wine that mankind has lived through, we fortunate few are the truly lucky ones, for we can count ourselves as being among the generation who are drinking in the Very Greatest Golden Age of Wine that mankind has ever witnessed.

But forgive me – we are rushing ahead of ourselves, like breathless teenagers clawing at one another's fasteners. Before I tell you about the Very Greatest Golden Age of Wine – My Age of Wine – there is so much of the rich, Claret-soaked tapestry of history to slowly and painstakingly unravel. So let us begin.

An example of early food and wine matching advice from a wine merchant in Lascaux: Bison with white wine, Mastodon with red wine.

Ancient times

Man has been making wine for well over 80,000 years. We know this because the naturally mummified remains of a Cro-Magnon vigneron were unearthed in the bilge below a London pizza restaurant in the early 1970s. Not only did the extraordinarily well-preserved specimen have red stained teeth, a breathalyser test (carried out by the ever-fastidious Metropolitan Police after the corpse refused to co-operate with their investigations) revealed that the mummified vigneron was still three times over the legal limit.

Further archaeological research revealed the startling fact that Norway is wine's pre-historic birthplace. Much of the early myth and legend surrounding wine is attached to the imperious figure of Odor, the God of Smelling, and Thor's twin brother. Odor is said to have judged at the first International Wine Challenge, assessing wine using his Riedel sword and shield. He had a gigantic nose, and Lappish oral traditions, such as the haunting 'Song of Cnut', suggest he had three nostrils.

The Old Testament

The Bible is the earliest and most impressive example of wine journalism in the Western Canon. The work is a masterful examination of the culture of the vine, as well as being a handy guide to the eradication of vineyard pests, and an extensive compilation of bawdy drinking songs.

This, for example, from Genesis, chapter 32:

> Binding his foal unto the vine,
> And his ass's colt unto the choice vine;
> He washed his garments in wine,
> And his clothes in the blood of grapes:
> His eyes shall be red with wine
> And his teeth white with milk.

This is obviously an early parable for malolactic fermentation.

Modern-day scholars have also demonstrated unquestionably that Noah's Ark came to rest not on Mount Ararat as has long been thought, but on the highest peak of the island of Madeira, confirming my belief that Madeira is not mere wine, but the very fluid of the Lord.

Noah's Ark.

The Greeks

The Wine Options game was invented at the infamous symposium made famous by Plato in his book, *The Republic*. You will remember that Socrates managed to persuade the great military commander and celebrated Athenian pisspot, Alcibiades, that rather than throwing the furniture into the street as Alcibiades was threatening to do (he was so drunk he was convinced he was on a sinking ship and needed to jettison the ballast), the men assembled for the symposium in the Andron (or 'men's room') should try and guess what wine was in Socrates' cup.

Things have hardly changed since the first Wine Option, except of course, that women are now occasionally allowed to play.

Typical painting from an ancient Greek drinking vessel, circa 400 BC.

The Romans

The Romans were the first to fully explore the concept of a multinational beverage company. At one stage, the Nerocorp Group had vineyards in all corners of the known world. Vast wineries staffed by slaves transported oceans of wine to Rome using the enormous network of viniducts built by the Imperial Legions. The Colosseum is, in fact, an old fermenting vat that was only transformed into an arena of death after the entire grape harvest of 63 BC was eaten by the invading Barbarian hordes.

In marked contrast to Nerocorp's vast enterprise, Rome was also surrounded by thousands of small vineyards – an eerie parallel to today's industry.

In 50 BC, Cicero, who was working tirelessly to preserve the crumbling principles of republicanism, instituted tax breaks for vineyard owners – establishing an early and very important precedent for the industry.

A famous Roman Emperor and CEO of Pilate Creek Wine Estates.

The New Testament

Jesus was not just a carpenter. He was, like his step-father, a cooper. And not just any old cooper, either: he was a cooper for Pilate Creek Wine Estates – one of the larger Roman wine companies.

The young Jesus, like many apprentices in his profession, was a heavy drinker and fervid moralist – especially on Friday nights. With his simple robes stuffed with a fat salary packet, Jesus and his chums – covered in sawdust and soot – would head off to the markets, get themselves awfully tipsy and overturn the tables of the wine merchants who ripped them off 'something chronic', as the apostle Luke was known to put it.

Many years later at the Last Supper, wine played a pivotal role in the unfolding drama. The terrible quality of the house wine caused the sommelier at the Garden of Gethsemane All-You-Can-Eat Food Barn, Judas, to leave that place in shame and hang himself (a lesson that perhaps some of today's wine waiters would do well to heed).

An early publicity picture of Jesus in the coopers' shop at Pilate Creek Wine Estates.

The Dark Ages

During the Middle Ages wine production and consumption flourished – as did the quality. Early Christian missionaries had taken the gentle art of wine-making to the far-flung reaches of the former Roman Empire – places such as Cork, Coventry and Calcutta.

These were dark days indeed for wine and its adherents.

But then: disaster. For some still-as-yet-unexplained reason, the people of Europe forgot how to make wine – consequently plunging the world into the Dark Ages. There is a poignant passage in Chaucer's *The Brewere's Tayle,* where the Nun tells the Bishop about how the grain has vanquished the grape:

This wyne of olde crepeth subtilly /In othere drynkes, growynge badde by, /Of which ther ryseth swich fumositee /That whan a man hath dronken draughtes thre, /And weneth that he dyd at the grounde vomitte, /He was cursynge all aboute the wynne, /Untyl myne hoste gav hym drafte ayle, /Sayinge Here be hayre of the hounde, /And he merrilye recoveryed immedyatelly.

It makes me weep to think of such times but, alas, we must move on.

Shakespeare

William Shakespeare was, without question, the finest wine writer the world has ever produced – the Oberon Kant of his day, if you like. In just three short years, this genius of the stage wrote a body of wine literature renowned for its invention of new language, iambic pentameter and wines under $10. But for the small fact of four centuries, I'm sure we would have been great mates.

His works are widely known but it is worth reflecting on a selection here – the mere invocation of his plays' titles is enough to lend gravitas to my humble pursuit:

- *Measure For Measure*: a manual for winemaking.
- *The Taming of the Brew*: a play about wine's resurgence after the Dark Ages.
- *The Wine Merchant of Venice:* including the famous line, 'this quality merlot is not strained'.
- *The Comedy of Errors:* a play about mistaking Burgundy for Bordeaux.

William Shakespeare, the world's most oft-quoted but completely misunderstood wine writer. I take my hat off to him.

Much Ado About Nothing: a guide to wine marketing.

The Merry Wines of Windsor: a catalogue of the royal cellar.

All's Well That End's Well: a damage-control guide to managing a wine scandal.

Further confirmation of Shakespeare's wine-writing prowess can be found in his remarkable wine-and-cigar matching plays *Hamlet*, and *Romeo and Juliet* – works that pre-date Marvin R. Shanken by more than 300 years.

The Eighteenth Century

The Eighteenth Century is not described as The Age of Rhenish for no reason. This was the period in history when God fell down to earth and was destroyed by science. Men ate and drank themselves into states of debilitating torpor as a result. Take as an example this passage from the diary of my ancestor, Doctor James Cantwell, a noted London wine merchant and literary scholar:

> March 20th, 1775: 'Comes my boy to tell me that the Duke of Wellington had sent for all the principal wine merchants, &c, to come to him today, so I went by water to Mr Avery's, and there staid and drank a good while on flagons of Rhenish, while downing a brace of pheasants and bottles of tiresome Madeira, until it were time to move into luncheon, where a fine Claret prompted Mr Keats to compose an ode while Mr Ruskin sketched the

scene so trippingly – 'tho, by his own admission, Mr Keats' rendition of his poem were so fierce that one of the ladies present – a Mrs Shelley, who had complained horribly of the Agues all morning – was forced to retire a-bed promptly, belching loudly, whereby the gentlemen moved to the sitting room to play cards and drink refreshing draughts of Port awhile, until I did return to my abode to meet with my boy and slake my raging thirst with more Claret and Hock and Madeira and some cheese before retiring to dinner.

My great mate, Samuel Johnson.

Phylloxera

In the 1840s tragedy befell the known world when the evil vine disease phylloxera devastated the vineyards of Burgundy and Madeira. Phylloxera is a fungus carried in the urine of vine-hugging marsupials that clogs up the petioles and can only be eradicated by the application of sun-dried tomatoes. However, this is knowledge safely viewed from the crucible of hindsight. Our poor, deluded ancestors tried every misguided trick in the book to combat the plague festering in their vines' roots before they found the cure.

Some vignerons had tried burning their vines – only to discover that the pathogens thrived on ash, redoubling in size and tripling in number the morning after the blaze. Some tried squirting the vines with cold coffee – a technique that had enjoyed limited success in Ireland during the famine (except coffee had been scarce there, so landowners used watered-down ink, which had no effect whatsoever, other than to blacken the otherwise light beige-coloured peat). Some even tried replanting their vines on phyl-

After mating, phylloxera urinate on the vines, dissolving the young tendrils.

loxera-resistant rootstock, but that led to a rapid diminution of quality, and was soon abandoned.

Eventually, after three decades of turmoil, every other vine in Europe had been destroyed – and thus, dear reader, was entrenched the practice, now all-too-common, of low-density vineyard planting – a practice which, I contend, is at the root of the spiritual and moral malaise among traditional winegrowing communities and, therefore, the world.

The modern era

If the modern era can be characterised by nothing else, then it is by the so-called 'popularisation of wine' – a trend that is directly related to my increasingly active involvement with the industry. Indeed, my career over the last thirty years exactly mirrors the progress of wine culture during the same time period.

I first worked on television in the 1960s, initially as a scriptwriter for Rowan and Martin's *Laugh-In*, then as a stand-in presenter for David Frost on *TWTWTW (That Was The Wine That Was)*. Such was my commanding screen presence that Barry Humphries based his now-famous character Tubby Grogan on me. As imitation is the highest form of flattery, I naturally took the portrayal as a compliment, even though Len Evans then pilfered that characterisation when he applied for his job at the Australian Wine Bureau (a jape that backfired as the poor bugger has had to remain in character ever since).

And so, here we are, in the present day, where young people are as comfortable with wine as it is with them.

Sometime during the 1970s, I think, I swiftly became the first syndicated wine writer in New Zealand, using my uncle's contacts from his days as *The Times'* wine correspondent during the Boer War. Indeed, I was the first to identify Blenheim and Marlborough as the Sauvignon Blanc capitals of the world – a feat that snared me the job as the first head of the New Zealand Wine Bureau, where I naturally did a great job. Indeed, I am proud to say that the average wine consumption in New Zealand had plummeted by the time I left.

After working as executive script editor on *Falcon Crest* in the very early 1980s (a position I simply could not maintain once audiences and the media realised that the character of Lance Cumson was loosely based on myself) I retired to my sheep station in Wangillialligong-on-Murray in South Australia – an idyllic spot I like to think of as my 'home' – to live the gentle life of an internationally acclaimed wine author and raconteur.

Notes

CHAPTER 2

How to taste wine PROPERLY

The seven steps of wine tasting: looking, listening, chewing, swallowing and so on and so forth.

I can't believe it's not butter!
PLINY THE ELDER

An awful lot of rot is written and spoken about wine tasting. As I will demonstrate in exhaustive detail, the average John and Jeffrey Smith in the High Street need not be in the slightest bit intimidated or alienated by what is essentially an accessible and low-risk spectator sport for all the family.

You will never be able to count yourself a true wine professional – or indeed, a lifelong amateur (in the very real sense) – unless you master the seven basic steps of wine tasting, appreciation and connoisseurship. I see young people entering the industry from behind these days and it makes me weep with pangs of nostalgia for what can only be described as wine's heyday, when respect and gratitude were an ambitious cellarman's most fervently prized emotional possessions.

The art and craft and science of wine tasting was first seriously developed in ancient Egypt by Pharaoh Eutypa III. This discovery was made in 1926 when I accompanied my great mate Howard Carter on one of his many bouts of wanton drunken destruction, rape and pillaging through the Valley of the Kings (ah, those were the days). Inscribed in great detail in full-colour bas-relief on the inside of Eutypa's sarcophagus was a wondrous account of his tasting notes – the first example of wine journalism, if you like. Ever since then, it has been my life's work to communicate what I saw to the world.

Reasons for tasting

These are many and varied, of course, for no one taster's objectives and thresholds can be deemed to be universally applicable or indeed homogenous. But whoever you are, whatever your social standing and level of experience, one eternal truth rings clear:

The art and craft and science of wine tasting exists to uphold vital critical and moral standards in society.

Remember to conduct yourself with complete decorum during a tasting.

Remember this: when you approach the tasting table you are at the vanguard of civilisation. Whether you be a wine professional or merely an interested amateur (in the very real sense), your performance in assessing each and every mouthful of ambrosial liquid is as crucial to the wellbeing of the mass of common humanity as is, say, the courageous and selfless work of an opposition spokesperson charged with the onerous burden of the aged care portfolio. Remember too, that by the time you leave the tasting table you could find yourself at the arse-end of civilisation unless you have conducted yourself with complete decorum during a tasting.

There is a myriad other reasons for tasting. For myself, there is a very strong religious dimension to the activity. I see being able to recognise the level of char of the barrels in which a particular Stellenbosch Cabernet Sauvignon has been aged as akin to penetrating the nexus between cool, sensible reason and the hot, life-giving forces of Bacchus himself. Wine tasting also:

- develops one's sensibilities;
- builds one's social confidence by giving one a kaleidoscope of conversational gambits;
- quenches thirst on a sultry summer's afternoon;
- passes the time satisfactorily between meals;
- stimulates the bowels.

Approaching one's wine

It is vitally important that wine tasting is approached in the right frame of mind. I have too often seen otherwise superb palates brought to their knees by a devilishly tricky glass of Yugoslav Laski Riesling simply because they were unable to leave behind them the stresses and strains of work, family life or a nagging mistress. I cannot over-emphasise this point strongly enough: one must have a clear, light and airy head when one tastes, and one's all-too-precious olfactory system – whether new, second-hand or hired especially for the occasion – must be regularly maintained to a high level of efficiency and willingness.

Here for the first time I reveal two essential tricks of the trade:

Self-love

I find that onanism is the most effective preparation for wine tasting. This may not always be practical, however, unless one is hosting the tasting, in which case popping off occasionally to readjust one's equilibrium is perfectly acceptable behaviour. Some of the world's best known wine identities – many of whom these days are women – practise this technique and report that they find it most relaxing. Indeed, without wishing to be so vulgar as to name names, certain female television wine personalities and Oxford Companion editors have been known to adjust themselves mentally at a crowded tasting at the Guildhall

Fine examples of institutional self-abuse from 18th century France.

by practising self-love AT THE SAME TIME AS writing eloquent and informative tasting notes. The logistics of such a task baffle me, but then I am a humble man, for whom the very concept of female infrastructure has always been a mysterious place (although I suspect that loose clothes designed by Issey Miyake play their part).

Reading poetry

Almost anything by Keats is perfect to calibrate one's organoleptic alertness. I find Ted Hughes and Seamus Heaney helpful before a tasting of aggressive young Barolos and Barbarescos. A quick skim through some Les Murray or Clive James is enormously focussing before a bracket of Australian Shiraz. The racier works of Sappho or e. e. cummings are terrific preparation for a mid-morning whip-through of the wines of the eastern Mediterranean islands. Pam Ayres and Spike Milligan should be avoided, however, unless one is obliged to attend one of those interminable tastings of sub-standard jug wine held by one of the less proactive supermarket chains every Friday out the back of the Sainsbury's loading bay on the Old Kent Road.

Points to observe

A bewildering array of distractions can conspire to seduce the taster away from his occupation. The taster must therefore learn to recognise and avoid such annoyances.

Smoking

If one must smoke at the tasting table, then one should attempt to avoid strongly aromatic tobacco products such as Indonesian cigarettes, stale Dominican half-coronas and marijuana – at least until after 10.00 a.m.

Company

A perennial question has emerged in the last six months that has caused much heated (but jovial) discussion in the Kant household: should women and men taste together? Some of the old stallions of the wine trade insist on a strictly male environment for wine tasting, arguing that the level of discussion is, by definition, trivialised when fillies are around. More enlightened souls, myself included of course, are of the

Women are infamous for disrupting serious wine tasting.

opinion that a woman – particularly if she is ovulating – can strangely alter the group dynamics of a wine tasting for the better. As my great mate, the late Harry Waugh, used to say: 'Before tasting the wine, taste the woman!' While somewhat off the point, this is great wisdom indeed. Harry was also of the opinion that if one can't find an ovulating woman, almost any other ovulating mammal will do – except koalas, which are notoriously vicious when ovulating.

Time

Allow hours and hours and hours for wine tasting. You will need a variety of naps during the day to focus your mind. Make sure comfortable chaise longues are available for all tasters, preferably in a darkened anteroom. Provide soft pillows and cashmere blankets, hot water bottles and mugs of Ovaltine.

Temperature

Researchers at the University of California at Davis have found that the temperature of the taster is in fact far more important than the temperature of the wine. Too cold, and the taster's olfactory system shuts down as surely as the engine of my beloved 1963 Austin Healey on a frosty morning. Too warm, and the sensitive bulb of nerve endings in the roof of the taster's sinus cavity engorge with blood and exaggerate any aromatic impressions, making insipid generic Beaujolais Villages taste like a Turley Zinfandel.

Attire

Checks, stripes, restrained floral prints and paisley are all acceptable forms of dress for a formal wine tasting. If the situation is less rigid then sports jackets, cufflinks, boob tubes, diaphanous frocks and body-hugging lycra twin sets are perfectly okay. Mambo or Tommy Hilfiger t-shirts, baggy cargo pants and sandals are frowned upon by polite society in most wine-producing nations. Combat gear is, apparently, not uncommon attire for wine tastings in Argentina. I myself have a range of invaluable antique bibs, hand-embroidered by vignerons' wives and daughters in the prettier villages of the Côtes de Jura, which my personal assistant delicately washes for me in neutral soap before each wine tasting. The appreciation of

Fine Wine can be a messy business, and one would not want to ruin one's tie – or anyone else's.

Physical Hazards

A number of things can creep up on the unwary taster and ruin his concentration. Watch out for the following:

- head colds;
- alcohol;
- wet suits;
- hard floors;
- earth-moving equipment with the keys in the ignition.

Avoid earth-moving equipment when tasting.

Before you start

It is essential that the keen wine-taster equip himself with at least all of the following – sparing no expense on seeking out the finest examples of each item. I suggest having a good scrounge through the world's great bazaars, where you will no doubt uncover priceless antiques. One can then ostentatiously display these antiquities in one's dining room and use with great flourish and braggadocio when intimidating guests at one's next dinner party.

Staff

An indispensable part of any wine-taster's armoury is a steady supply of willing but unambitious staff. Opening bottles, arranging and washing glasses, stocking the cellar with unopened product samples and roasting the ducks are all tasks that are much more efficiently undertaken by one's assistants – leaving oneself free to concentrate on wine's infinite multifariousness.

Discretion is essential in hired help.

I recommend at least four permanent helpers: a cork-screwer, a pourer, a blind-folder and a masseuse. One should also be adequately equipped with a bevy of casuals ('runners' as they're known in the trade). If you cannot coerce your loved ones or strangers encountered on park benches at dusk into helping you, then you can hire staff for reasonable rates from Mousetrap and Kant Recruitment Services, the world's leading wine-industry supplier of freshly scrubbed young oenology graduates (visit www.mousekanteers.com for details).

Corkscrews

These are much more than an implement with which one extracts corks from bottles. The corkscrew is the wine-taster's trusted and reliable friend, an heirloom for future generations, and an object of great beauty. Look for a corkscrew with a very sharp serrated knife attachment (ideal for cutting off slices of chorizo or blue cheese to accompany one's wine tasting). One's corkscrew should also have a chain or fanciful ribbon so that one can hang it round one's neck in the fashion of the Sommeliers du Confrérie du Chevaliers du Bouchon, whose work I admire immensely. Look, too, for a corkscrew with an ivory handle (preferably intricately carved with erotic designs by Polynesian craftsmen) or rare Brazilian rainforest hardwood. It is essential to inherit a sabre to remove stubborn champagne corks,

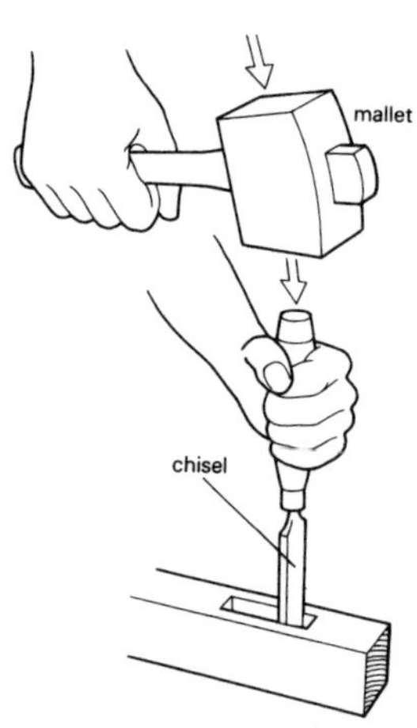

Traditional corkscrews are best.

and a pair of Port tongs and mobile furnace for opening bottles of crusted Port or Madeira. I purchase most of my openers – and naturally I have an extensive array – from Pieter de Kanter's Antique Wine Accessories Emporium in Johannesburg. Pieter has a thriving mail-order business and can be contacted by email at tastevin@dekanter.co.za.

Glasses

These need to be as large as possible. There is absolutely no point whatsoever in using those pathetic little so-called International Standards Organisation tasting glasses – they don't hold nearly enough wine as needs to be consumed and they break far too easily when you tap them against the table to hear the wine's ringing note (an essential part of the wine tasting process – see below). No, you need vast, fish-bowl-sized drinking vessels. I find that customised eighteenth century lead crystal chamber pots do the trick admirably – in fact, far from getting in the way, the handles are very useful for lifting the vessel to one's ear. The extensive Oberon Kant Collection of excellent glassware – including exquisite reproduction chamber pots crafted for me personally by a family of Czech glass blowers – is available from Bludgeon Brothers and Kant, Wine Merchants at No. 3, The Strand, London SW3.

Decanters

While I adore the shimmering beauty of a 50-year-old First Growth, full of gustatory anticipation in a crystal decanter on the mantelpiece, each facet of the glass reflecting the candlelight as a jewel-like glimpse of the garnet-coloured liquid inside, I must confess that my favourite vessel for decanting and breathing wine is the pith helmet. A nostalgic remnant of my days in the Third Punjabi Jabbers, the pith helmet's wide proportions and perfect 750 ml capacity is exceptional for the aeration of wine. This aeration can be aided immeasurably by a few swift rounds from your trusty Browning, fired directly into the deepest point of the liquid. Reasonably priced pith helmets can be obtained from Raj Disposals in Colonial Avenue, Calcutta. Ask for Rajid Kant – a distant cousin of mine.

Cards

Essential for recording one's impressions of each wine, tasting cards can be as small as postage stamps and as large as mainsails – depending on one's verbosity. For my tasting cards, I use betting slips that I buy in bulk at an extraordinary saving. I have filing cabinets full of intricately cross-referenced slips (some beginning to yellow and go brittle at the edges) chronicling my decades of tasting experience. Recording tasting notes on betting slips can, incidentally, yield unexpected results: I managed to win the trifecta at the 1993 Melbourne Cup with a brief description of a Hunter Valley Chardonnay. Tasting notes can be purchased from Freddy Kant's Gambling Warehouse (phone Freddy on 0796 121 121 – confidentiality assured) or your local bookmaker.

Table and Chair

These are not essential items for the dedicated taster. I have hosted perfectly agreeable wine tastings from the back of an orange Volvo Estate. Indeed, my great mate Michael Parkinson and I once raised £200 3s at an impromptu charity wine tasting for 11,000 opera lovers at Glyndebourne armed with nothing more than a few jumping sticks, an upturned picnic hamper and half a dozen multicoloured anodised aluminium salad bowls. It was the quality of the wine, you see, which was all that mattered (if memory serves me correctly, the wine was a particularly fine shipment of non-vintage Pol Roger). But if you must install a permanent table and chair arrangement, then I must insist upon teak. It doesn't stain quite as permanently as the other hardwoods, and is relatively aroma-free. Purchases can be made from the fine purveyors at Kant & Co. Exotic Timbercarvers, located in the industrial park on the outskirts of Newcastle. Tremendous prices for timeless workmanship.

Dog

In these days of ever-increasing accusations that wines can be tainted by the corks that seal them (claims that I unhesitatingly refute and ascribe to the band of Labor-voting agitators at the Australian Wine Research Institute), and the very real problem of screw-cap-closure-taint, I find more and more professional tasters and amateurs (in the very real sense) are employing the services of a tasting hound. The hound – preferably a short-haired Airedale – is sent into the room where the tasting is to take place and will sniff each bottle, savaging any sommelier who dares serve less-than-perfect wine. Fully-trained and child-friendly tasting hounds are available through K&K Airedales, Kantalong Lane, Yarrambat (open the first Sunday of each month, October to April, 10.00 a.m.–3.00 p.m.).

The art and craft and science of tasting wine

Here we move swiftly onto the most important section of this chapter in this book. I will explain the seven steps of wine tasting in detail, so you will need to pay particular attention, and may even need to read the next few paragraphs over and over again until tasting becomes as instinctive as breathing, talking or shooting.

Step 1: Look at the wine

An enormous amount of information about a wine's quality can be gleaned by simply looking at it. After you have stared at the label for a while, you may then want to see the bottle's contents. To do this, carefully pour the wine into a clean, fresh and odour-free glass, making sure your assistant has opened the bottle first (an invaluable piece of advice given to me by the late, great André Simon, who had a reputation in wine circles for frequently flying into a blind rage when unable to pour a fragile old Burgundy because the cork was still in). Make sure you pour the wine all the way up to the rim of the glass (filling it completely), or you will be unable to measure the precise refractive index of the liquid. Now carefully tear a page from the A–K volume of the telephone directory or Peter Carey's *True History of the Kelly Gang* and tape it carefully to the side of the glass facing away from you. Take the glass to a south-east-facing window and look through it. If you can read the text from one side of the page through the wine, the wine is Fine. If you can read both sides of the page clearly, the wine is Very Fine. If you can see nothing at all because a) the wine is too opaque or b) the curtains are drawn, then the wine is, without doubt, Very Fine Indeed. (For an explanation of these tasting terms, see the introduction situated at the front of this book.)

Step 2: Listen to the wine

Pour about a third of the contents of your glass into a large porcelain tray in which you have previously placed a jointed chicken, a few cloves of garlic, some peppercorns and a sprig of fresh thyme (this marinade can also be used for other breeds of poultry such as emu, rabbit and button mushrooms). Take your now-two-thirds-full glass and gently tap it against the edge of the tasting table or whatever surface you are employing for the exercise (be careful of Volvo bumper bars, however, as they are unforgiving on even the toughest glassware). As the wine resonates with its own distinctive tone, hold the glass to your ear – *'écoute du vin!'* – as my great mate and tasting mentor Professor Emile Peynaud used to scream at his students. This stage of the tasting process can be remarkably useful for determining a wine's provenance: the gentle sound of rolling surf, for example, indicates the wine is from a classic maritime region such as Champagne or Margaret River; the persistent thump of an oompah band and the wine is undoubtedly from the Barossa Valley or the Mosel; the seductive growl of a brand new BMW immediately gives the wine away as coming from the Napa Valley or the Mornington Peninsula.

Such is my skill at identifying a wine's quality by sound alone that I am frequently telephoned by winemakers across the globe and asked for advice. The winemaker will hold the phone handset next to a tank of fermenting must while a cellar-hand drops a river pebble into the foaming liquid. The sound of the stone's 'plop!' is enough for me to not only gauge the grape variety and alcohol level, but to also accurately predict whether the wine will win any medals at the *Concours Mondiale du Vins et Spiriteaux* in Brussels, of which I am president. 'Vertical tasting' is the term we wine professionals use to describe this part of the process conducted while standing up.

Step 3: Smell the wine

By now, your staff should have rolled up a few banknotes lengthwise into nostril-width straws, fastened using rust-proof staples or hypoallergenic organic glue. (Your own staff will soon become adept at rolling notes to exactly the right proportions. They may have to experiment with different currencies, although from personal experience I find plastic rather than paper money works best.) Dip two of these 'straws' into the wine and gently insert the exposed ends into your nose. The next stage may take some practice: the trick is to sniff the wine up the straws just far enough so that it touches the sensitive nostril hairs right at the opening of your nasal passages. Try this out a few times at home with Coca Cola, bleach or some other low-grade irritant, and you will soon get the hang of it (this is based on a crude but effective form of aversion therapy my great mate Tim Hanni developed on the Mondavi Wine Education Program in the early 1970s). The idea is to bring the volatile odorous molecules of the wine as close as possible to the protective lipoid coating of the olfactory epithelium. 'Horizontal tasting' is the term we wine professionals use to describe this part of the process conducted while lying down.

Dedicated tasters may wish to experiment with what is known in the trade as 'extreme tasting' by inserting the straws all the way into the nostrils, past the turbinate bones and cribriform plate, piercing the olfactory bulb itself and making direct contact with the trigeminal nerve. A warning, however: this practice can be dangerous. Such undiluted experience with Very Fine Wines – the 1971 Penfolds Grange, say – has been known to cause nausea and fainting in less-experienced tasters.

Step 4: Chew the wine

Tip your head forward slightly, open your mouth, jut out your chin and have one of your staff pour the wine in a long, continuous motion in the trough-like retention area you have created between your lower lip and bottom front teeth until the glass is empty. Keeping your mouth wide open, roll your head slowly backwards, then sideways, then forwards again, repeating the procedure in a rocking motion until the wine has covered every square inch of your gums, tongue, palate, and mouth. (This is where I find my hand-embroidered bibs most useful.) You need to distribute the wine evenly over all four sets of tastebuds – the circumvallate papillae, the filiform papillae, the foliate papillae and last but not least, the fungiform papillae – each of which is charged with sensing the various taste elements of wine: sweetness, sourness, quality, alcohol, salinity, breeding, resentment, playfulness and 'tsunami' (the controversial Japanese 'seventh samurai of the tastes', which roughly translates as 'stultifying turgidness in autumn').

Once evenly distributed, the taster must then vigorously masticate, working the wine in his mouth into a foam, thus neatly bringing the circle of life as initiated by fermentation to a satisfying conclusion. 'Comparative tasting' is the term we wine professionals use to describe chewing more than one wine at a time.

The famous antipodean wine writer and raconteur Walter James was, at the height of his career, able to masticate seven wines concurrently – without spilling a single drop. Indeed, he toured the United States during the Depression performing this feat to rapturous crowds at public wine tasting demonstrations.

Step 5: Swallow the wine

Neither as simple, as easy or as innocuous as it sounds, swallowing is a crucial step in the full appreciation of wine. One must swallow the foaming mouthful of thoroughly masticated wine as slowly and as thoughtfully as possible, fully registering how the wine caresses the bronchial papillae at the back of the throat. Imagine you are reclining in a Parisian bordello in the late nineteenth century, and the madam is carefully inserting a four-foot-long peacock's tail into your mouth and down your throat as she puffs suggestively on a black Russian cigarette. This sensation is referred to as the 'length' or 'finish' of the wine and should be as complex as possible, often lasting for 60 seconds or more. This is where truly great wines or

Grand Vins shine – in the length of the peacock's tail and the intensity of the scent of the bordello. All practised wine-tasters carry a stopwatch and wooden ruler for measuring this finish. Indeed, I have had the privilege of tasting a sixteenth century Trockenbeerenauslesen with a finish that lasted a full fourteen months and six inches. (Some modern exponents of the art, craft and science of wine tasting advocate spitting. I find this practice only useful if one wants to confirm one's initial impressions of the wine retronasally – that is, on the way out.)

L. ANNÆI
SENECÆ
PHILOSOPHI
OPERA, QVÆ EXSTANT
OMNIA:
A IVSTO LIPSIO
emendata, et Scholijs illustrata

Step 6: The tasting note

The final and most important part of the wine tasting process is the recording of accurate, evocative and concise tasting notes for the wine in question. Communicating the aroma and taste of wine to others is a skill that can only be perfected through years of experience and learning – or by reading authoritative scholarly treatises such as this. Here are some pointers to efficient wine descriptions:

- One must use precise and accurate tasting terminology in one's descriptions – words such as 'serpentine', 'lackadaisical' and 'stodgy', for example, are all perfectly fine – unless one is alone, in which case pictograms, charcoal smudges and the use of bodily fluids as a medium of expression are entirely acceptable.

- If one is tasting in public, one's opinions of a wine must be formulated quickly and defended vigorously until one is forced off the stage by a barrage of rotten vegetables.

- One must identify and criticise a wine mercilessly if one detects a fault or dip in performance from one vintage to the next, or a typographical error on the back label. The producer must then be pilloried at every available opportunity until he (or she) goes out of business or one is forced off the stage by a barrage of rotten vegetables.

- Above all, one must keep levity to a minimum and brevity to a maximum. We are, after all, practising a science, an art and a craft. This is serious work and should be approached accordingly – unless one is forced off the stage by a barrage of rotten vegetables.

Let me show you how to put these principles into practice. The following is an example of a tasting note for a Wehlennenuhr Spatzburgunden Faulehringer Spatlese Trocken – one of the finest Rieslings produced in the hills of New Caledonia. It was written by one of the new breed of spiky-haired popular young wine identities:

> Clear as a bell and almost water-white with flashes of green, this excellent young Riesling has pure, pristine citrus fruit and floral, blossom aromas, is crisp and refreshing in the mouth, and finishes with a long, zingy twist of

> lime-zest. Delicious now and should age well for five to ten years. Rush out and buy some.

This is, of course, absolute twaddle and of practically no use to the average reader who, thirsty for information, is left none the wiser as to what this wine might taste like, how good it might be, or whether or not he or she should buy some.

Here, in stark contrast, is my tasting note for the same wine:

> Once as a lad I took a summer off from the hustle and bustle of city life at Oxford, and wandered through the Georgian steppes, pausing every few days at one of the many roadside inns, knowing full well that my every need would be met by the strapping lasses of the region. As I left each place – my heart a little larger, my purse a little lighter – a garland of wildflowers would be draped ceremoniously around my neck by the loveliest of the inn-keeper's daughters. When the flowers on each garland began to wither and die, their fresh scent giving way to the pungent but alluringly sweet odour of decay, I knew it was time to pause once more and break my journey at the next inn.
>
> 🍷 ☠☠☠ Very Fine. 37/50. Gold and a half.
> Drink: 1986.

I think you'll agree that there is simply no comparison.

For a comprehensive list of tasting terms, see the glossary at the back of this book. There are also some very useful tools available to the interested wine-taster such as diagrammatical representations of the families of taste and flavour to be found in wine. These include the Aroma Wheel, developed by Ann and Al Noble at UC Davis; the Mouth Feel Wheel, developed by the AWRI in China; the Mood Swing Pendulum, developed by the Australian Women's Winemakers Institute in McLaren Vale; and the Wine-Taster's Internal Thermometer, designed by Dr B. Halifax of the University of the South Pacific. All can be ordered through my website, www.oberonkant.com.au.

JUDGING AND CRITICISING WINE – TASTING THE PROFESSIONAL WAY

As a wine professional, you will inevitably be called upon to judge at one of the many wine competitions that take place around the globe each week. This is an honour and a privilege – and should never be treated lightly. Your chance to reward greatness and castigate mediocrity will be one of the most satisfying experiences of your young life. As an extra incentive, you will also visit the great wine regions of the world and become intimate with a large number of like-minded wine professionals, both in the heat of the tasting room and afterwards among the convivial camaraderie of the post-tasting dinner and, after that, over Port and cigars and, after that, in the billiards room and, after that, in the hotel sauna – all at the expense of your generous hosts, the wine competition's organising committee. If such good fortune should befall you, it is advisable to remember that different cultures approach the solemn business of wine judging in sometimes starkly diverse ways.

This entails wearing a white coat; scribbling one's tasting notes on a clipboard; tasting 3000 competently made but ultimately unexciting six-month-old Chardonnays before breakfast; arguing half-heartedly with the other judges about the merits of wine 16 in class 5; drinking Coopers Pale Ale by the keg-full and sleeping with the associate judges and/or stewards. International guest judges are also required to make gently self-deprecating and mildly critical speeches at interminable judges' dinners where the local vignerons and their families dress up in ill-fitting tuxedos and sit around small tables in sagging marquees in soggy paddocks and shovel down plates groaning with innovative regional modern Australian cuisine and drink as much of the trophy-winning wines as they can fit into their bloated bellies.

This entails wearing a white coat; scribbling one's tasting notes on a clipboard; tasting 3000 competently made but ultimately unexciting six-month-old Sauvignon Blancs before breakfast; arguing half-heartedly with the other judges about the merits of wine 16 in class 5; drinking Steinlager by the keg-full and sleeping with the associate judges, the stewards and the regional PR girl. International guest judges are also required to make slightly self-deprecating but somewhat critical speeches at interminable judges' dinners where the local vignerons and their families dress up in ill-fitting tuxedos and sit around small tables in sagging marquees in soggy paddocks and shovel down plates groaning with innovative regional modern New Zealand cuisine and drink as much of the trophy-winning wines as they can fit into their bloated bellies.

This entails wearing a white coat; scribbling one's tasting notes on a clipboard; tasting 3000 competently made but ultimately unexciting six-month-old Zinfandels before breakfast; arguing half-heartedly with the other judges about the merits of wine 16 in class 5; drinking seasonal ale from the local micro-brewery by the keg-full and sleeping with the associate judges, the stewards and the regional PR boy. International guest judges are also required to make witty and ever-so-slightly critical speeches at interminable judges' dinners where the local vignerons and their families dress down in loud shirts and sandals and sit around small tables in sagging marquees in soggy paddocks and shovel down plates groaning with innovative regional modern Californian cuisine and drink mineral water.

This entails wearing a white coat; scribbling one's tasting notes on a clipboard; tasting 3000 competently made but ultimately unexciting six-month-old Pinotages before breakfast; arguing half-heartedly with the other judges about the merits of wine 16 in class 5; drinking Carling Lager by the keg-full and going to bed early. International guest judges are also required to make extremely self-deprecating and entirely uncritical speeches at interminable judges' dinners where the local vignerons and their families dress up in ill-fitting tuxedos and sit around small tables in sagging marquees in soggy paddocks and shovel down plates groaning with innovative regional modern South African cuisine and drink as much of the trophy-winning wines as they can fit into their bloated bellies.

This entails wearing a white coat; scribbling one's tasting notes on a clipboard; tasting fifteen badly made but occasionally drinkable sixteen-year-old Madirans before lunch; arguing half-heartedly with the other judges about the Quebec question; drinking Armagnac from the bottle at midnight in the town square and sleeping with the associate judges, the stewards, the regional PR boy and girl and the mayor's daughter. International guest judges are a rare sight at interminable judges' dinners where the local vignerons and their families dress in their Sunday best and sit around small tables in sagging marquees in soggy paddocks and shovel down plates groaning with dull regional cuisine and drink as much Pastis and Armagnac as they can fit into their bloated bellies.

This entails turning up just after lunch; scribbling one's tasting notes on the back of an envelope; tasting three or four dozen rather lacklustre Reichensteiners before tea; arguing passionately with the other judges about the merits of the *Telegraph's* new wine columnist; drinking Champagne and sleeping with one's secretary. International guest judges are also required to listen to gently self-deprecating and mildly critical speeches at interminable judges' dinners where the local merchants and their families dress up in ill-fitting tuxedos and sit around small tables in sagging hotels and shovel down plates groaning with innovative regional modern Australian cuisine and drink as much of the after dinner Port as they can fit into their bloated bellies.

Judging: Upholding Critical Values

After serving many years of an apprenticeship – first as a steward, then an associate judge, then a chairman of judges and then a charity wine auctioneer – the wine professional can apply to the Wine Writer's Association of National Confederations to become a fully-accredited wine journalist, critic and author. This should be the ultimate goal for any aspiring amateur (in both the very real and vaguely imagined sense).

If the function of tasting wine is to uphold vital critical and moral standards in society, then the role of the wine writer is to spearhead the moral vanguard. In our writings, we in the wine media have a crucial role to play in moulding future generations. It is a responsibility that I bear with pride, dignity and a not insignificant amount of joy.

As a wine journalist, critic and author, there are three special considerations I must bring to the tasting table:

1. The Role of the Journalist

One must always be on the lookout for glaring errors and omissions of fact (not to mention outright lies) in the wine industry. Without the vigilant eyes of the wine media, errant apostrophes and confused compliments will run riot on the back labels of bottles across the globe – corrupting young minds and eroding the very fabric of the international wine trade.

2. The Role of the Critic

One must be fearless in one's criticism of wine. If one finds fault, then one must say so, just as one should be compelled to praise excellence from the rooftops – unless, of course, one is shown a jolly good time by the producer's PR company, jetted off to Italy for wining and dining up and down the Amalfi coast and put up in first-class resorts before being packed off with a few dozen mementos of one's visit. In such cases, one must naturally endeavour to bring a balanced view to one's weekly recommendations. Better still, the opportunity to do some quiet ghost writing for the same PR company is never unwelcome.

3. The Role of the Author

One must never forget that one is, first and foremost, telling a story in one's writing. If a tasting note can't have a beginning, a middle and an ending (and a happy ending at that) then what hope have the rest of us mere mortals struggling to be heard, struggling to be recognised in this often harsh and brutal glimpse of life on earth?

Wine parties – tasting [in a very real sense] as an amateur

In recent years, it has become *de rigueur* in some of the more fashionable parts of West London and San Francisco to hold what is colloquially referred to as a 'tasting party'. I have attended a few in my time – most notably a recent four-day affair hosted by my

A simple, intimate wine party with a few friends makes an enjoyable evening.

great mate Harvey Birkenstock, the Florida entrepreneur and billionaire, whose passion for pre-phylloxera magnums of Lafleur Petrus is prodigious, and whose generosity is legendary. I have found such tasting parties most agreeable.

To hold a tasting party at one's own residence, one need only assemble a dozen or so wines – the identity of which should be suitably obscured by one's staff (silver foil is perfect for wrapping tightly around each bottle, but some continental wine-producing regions retain the quaint habit of masking the bottles in a vine-pruner's sock – a practice which, one can't help feeling, must impact on the varietal definition of the wine being offered for tasting, but I digress).

One then gathers friends and family and seats the party around one's largest circular dining table. Each wine is poured in succession and the host – that would be you – asks a series of questions about the wine, from which an amusing array of answers ensues. Good questions include:

1 How big is this wine?
2 If I paid six pounds ninety-nine for it (I didn't, it cost me considerably more than that, but for the sake of argument let's say I did) how much would I have to pay in a wine shop in Seville in two years' time?
3 Is this wine from the Old World, or not?
4 Was this wine made by a woman, a man, or a machine?
5a How many points did this wine garner from the Wine Spectator in 1986?
5b Was it this vintage?
6a Who won the Oscar for best supporting actress in 1986?
6b No, it wasn't Sissy Spacek – why not?
7 How many more bottles of this wine have I got in my cellar?

The winner of this enormously exciting game is the last one left awake at the end of the evening. Novice hosts should bear in mind that informality, intimacy and the sense of relaxed confidence usually engendered in participants of a wine tasting party can result in outbreaks of mass mutual onanism. It is therefore advisable to have plenty of Kleenex on hand.

CHAPTER 3

A definitive guide to the grapes

All the world's great grapes and wine styles explained in magnificent, evocative, spine-tingling, mouth-watering, Rabelaisian detail.

Variety is the spice of life.
HENRY FORD

Wine is made from grapes. Some grapes are better than others – a lot like people, really. It's all about breeding and location: location, location, location. Quality people tend to do quite well for themselves in any area, of course, but quality people in a quality area – such as Buckinghamshire, for instance – tend to do very well indeed. It is of no minor coincidence that the best Burgundy is made in Burgundy. Pinot Noir is made in other areas in other countries, but it is not Burgundy at all – and there lies the problem.

But the grapes. They come in bunches picked by people that one employs during the late summer or early autumn. Sometimes a machine can be used to pick the grapes from the plants upon which they grow, but none of my friends do that.

Burgundy is the best grape, followed by Bordeaux, which can be white or red or even Beaujolais-coloured wine. Rhone grapes can also be quite useful when serving barbecued meats [see Chapter 10: Wine and Food]. Riesling is very good to Quite Fine, but only when drunk in Germany. Spanish wine is not made from grapes at all, but bull's blood, pork fat and paprika – not too bad as a quaffer. South American wine has not been any good since my great mate Augusto Pinochet got himself discharged, but gosh we've had some wonderful dinners together over the years.

There are other grapes in the New World, including my adopted homeland, Australia. They have Chardonnay there, which the local women drink while their menfolk guzzle beer. There is also Shiraz, which is a red wine that tastes a little like Port made in the Rhone Valley – if you can imagine such an appalling mutation. Semillon is another variety, but it is actually an incorrectly labelled Riesling.

The grape

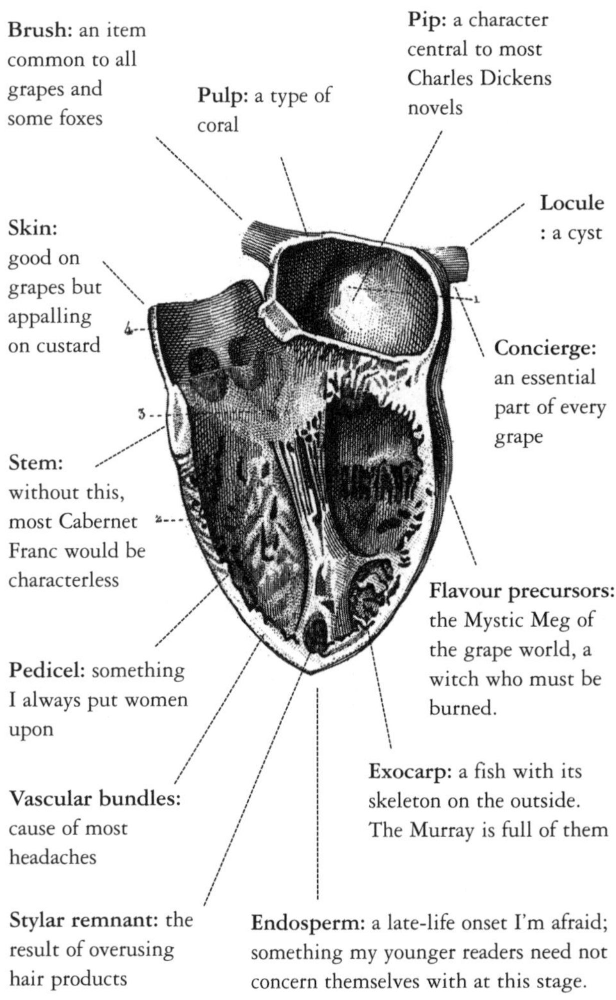

Brush: an item common to all grapes and some foxes
Pulp: a type of coral
Pip: a character central to most Charles Dickens novels
Locule : a cyst
Skin: good on grapes but appalling on custard
Concierge: an essential part of every grape
Stem: without this, most Cabernet Franc would be characterless
Flavour precursors: the Mystic Meg of the grape world, a witch who must be burned.
Pedicel: something I always put women upon
Exocarp: a fish with its skeleton on the outside. The Murray is full of them
Vascular bundles: cause of most headaches
Stylar remnant: the result of overusing hair products
Endosperm: a late-life onset I'm afraid; something my younger readers need not concern themselves with at this stage.

Ethnic words for the grape

As wine is made in every country of the world in which my readers may find themselves, I feel compelled to alert them to various cultures' most important word. Memorise these and you will never go thirsty.

French – *Raisin*
Italian – *Uva*
German – *Rebe*
Polynesian – *Cava*
American – *Merlot*
Scottish – *Oat*
Chinese – *Additive 621*
Australian – *Efficiency gain*

Wine: good grapes and those of lesser quality

Champagne

All Champagne is good to Very Fine. It is usually made from any white grape and chalk, except in Spain where white asparagus is used.

White wine

White Burgundy and white Bordeaux are quite good. They are made from local French grapes.

Red wine

Burgundy grapes and Bordeaux grapes are Very Fine. Pinot Noir and Cabernet are international grape varieties – rendering them morally affronting.

Port

Made from autochthonous Portuguese fruits. Excellent.

Madeira

Made from Portuguese fruits grown on a tropical island. Outstanding.

Sauvignon Blanc

Is not a grape but a noxious weed. I am the honorary president for a society (the name of which escapes me) dedicated to its destruction. Reports that my former great mate Saddam Hussein is in possession of – and threatening to use – Sauvignon Blanc as a weapon of mass destruction are in no way far-fetched.

Sherry

This is made from old sticks and twigs. Grapes only ruin the flavour.

Synthetic grapes

Grapes from which wines are made in the New World. Quite justifiably, the wines are sealed with stelvin caps. A cynical marketing ploy aimed at Generation X, whatever that is.

Genetically modified grapes

An outstanding breakthrough in which I have played no small part. My great mates at Monsanto have allowed me to push the boundaries of grapes' natural qualities. By inserting my own genes into a grape I have, in some small way, been able to give something back to the industry that has fed and watered me so well for so long. The Kant Cross is remarkably thick-skinned and will thrive under all conditions. It is the only grape in the world to have two stomachs.

Other uses for grapes

Brandy: a great wine.
Neutral grape spirit: the essence of the grape. An outstanding luncheon wine.
Verjus: a sweet dessert wine.
Vinegar: a much too sweet dessert wine.
Cooking: something that is increasingly done on television since the demise of journalism.
Tartaric acid: a low-kilojoule coffee sweetener.

Chapter 4

Where wine comes from

Getting dirt under one's fingernails – in the vineyard, in the rain and the hail, very occasionally.

Never root Daphne in a wet bed, but always have Ivy up against the wall.

Benjamin Hill, Kew Gardens, 1973

And on the eighth day God made wine. Well, as a matter of fact, He didn't. The Lord was not an oenologist as such, but rather a viticulturist. Yes, rather big words I know. Please allow me to explain. As the vicar said to the chorus girl, this will not take a minute.

An oenologist makes wine – or, at least, used to. It is even alleged that oenologists made wines in Burgundy as recently as the 1950s. Winemakers, in the old-fashioned sense, were wonderful, salt-of-the-earth types who actually made wine. The new, contemporary lot of oenologists – the promoters – merely want to go drinking with journalists all the time. They hope that this will be enough to guarantee some sort of media coverage, including a photograph of the said winemaker on his vineyard manager's tractor or with his cellar-hand's dog. A few glossy magazine pages later and this hybrid promoter–winemaker imagines himself the ruler of the world. They start travelling first class hither and thither at the drop of a hat – telling their staff and loved ones that the job nowadays requires this sort of promotional activity.

And they are right. The most diligent of this new breed of winemaker can often be found far from home, late at night, in a strange, foreign city, talking animatedly to young waitresses or any other young girl who is lucky enough to be in the vicinity, about the ways, means and hotel mini-bars of the global wine industry. And while this is vital work – more vital than even you, dear reader, could ever imagine – none of it could take place if not for the viticulturists; the chaps who make vines grow and subsequently (often within just a few weeks) bear grapes. They do this in any kind of climate (often climates totally unsuited to vines), in any kind of soil (often soils that are, in fact, not even soils), at any expense (usually high to very high to impossibly high, and best of all – bankrupting), and for reasons that completely mystify most of their friends, families, accountants, captains of industry, other vignerons, the press, the local community, internationally recognised experts, and the United Nations.

As a result of all this hard work and great vision, the global citizens of the world can now proudly say they live in the titanium-mounted, lapis lazuli-encrusted Golden Age of Wine. And wine, as this clearly shows – if I may coin a phrase – starts in the vineyard.

It requires two men, both with sticks, to beat a vineyard into shape.

Planting a vineyard

Furniture

To begin with, one needs some posts. You buy these at a local timber supplier. Treated pine posts are popular, as are steel posts, or even ones made from recycled materials – but I have always thought it miserly to establish a vineyard with second-hand goods. The posts go into the ground, usually in straight lines, at intervals of, say, 20–30 feet. A depth of six inches or so is enough, for they serve no other purpose than to let tourists know that they are driving past a vineyard. The tourist then tends to slow down, come into your cave or cellar door and taste your wine in a very serious and mostly uneducated way before buying the two worst wines you have. So posts, as I think I have quite neatly demonstrated, are invaluable.

Poplar posts, popular in Piedmont, are promtly punted down the Po prior to planting.

Once the posts are in, you may be struck by the rather dreary aspect they afford – particularly from the road on which the tourist is travelling. Vines can now be employed to help beautify the scene, lending a sort of rustic, bucolic feel to the general environment. You will need to prune the vines every year and water them heavily in the hotter months to promote vigour and leafy, verdant foliage. This is where the viticulturist comes into play.

The expert consultant

Have a viticulturist appoint vineyard staff to tend the vines. This will ease his burden and provide him with the necessary time to spend telephoning bulk wine suppliers hunting down the best-value bulk wine currently doing the rounds. Sometimes it takes just one phone call and your cellar is full to the gunwales with super premium wine in every style imaginable – all ready to be promoted by your winemaker all over the globe, late at night, in hotel rooms lit only by the dim glow of the slightly ajar door of an empty bar-fridge. But this is not to suggest that great wine can be made anywhere. No, no, no.

Terroir

Great wine can only be made in the already established and established-beyond-any-doubt and established-for-reasons-which-are-God-given regions of the world. Such as Burgundy. Or Alsace and Madeira. Bordeaux isn't bad either. The wines – and I use the term wine here rather loosely – of the New World have never, are never and never will ever, ever be great. This is because they are not grown in Burgundy. If New World wine producers showed any hint of innovation or intelligence they would buy some land in Burgundy and make their ghastly wine there. This may appear sacrosanct, but at least the subsequent beverage would be palatable.

As a general rule one needs a pretty view in order to produce great wine. If one is proficient in the use of photographic apparatus, one can then take a range of delightful pictures of the vineyard which may subsequently be used to add some charm to one's label. Views also bring in the tourist – without which most vignerons would not survive from one overseas trip to the next.

Soon this will be a vineyard. Alas all things must pass.

Vineyards should also be planted handy to good accommodation; cafes; at least two decent restaurants (not including the restaurant attached to one's own winery); a school; public transport; shops; an international airport; a major sporting venue; a cathedral independently dated no later than the sixteenth century, and a betting track. These combined local amenities are known in France as 'terroir'.

Driveways are also terribly important. The best are not necessarily paved or sealed, but offer the tourist the sense of some 4WD adventure without the inconvenience of potholes, river crossings, mud, undulations of any kind, corrugated surfaces, gravel, stone-chips, or broken windscreens. Terracotta-coloured Astro-Turf or Rebound Ace is ideal. A great winery producing great wines will have a driveway at least twenty-three miles long. (The driveway of my great mate Robert Mugabe's winery starts in Zimbabwe and finishes on the outskirts of a little village near Carcassonne. His wine is, needless to say, superb.)

Caring for the bio-diversity of your vineyard

Also critical to the vineyard are companion or 'indicator' plants. Traditionally, vignerons have chosen roses to plant at the end of each row of vines. The myth was that when the vineyard was about to explode in a ball of flame and toxic gas, the roses would chirp – thus alerting the winemaker and his media guests to the coming peril and enabling them to escape to the safety of a nearby bar. But myth was all that it was.

Recent research undertaken by the Oberon Kant Professor for Viticultural Innovation at Davis has clearly shown that the best companion plant for vineyards anywhere in the world is bamboo. My own vineyards have been planted in this way since the early 1970s. Not only do they produce superb fruit, but also encourage the healthy proliferation of the micro-bio-sphere, by which of course I mean panda. Baby panda – when treated as one would a spatchcock – is the best eating in the world, and one eats baby panda knowing one is doing Mother Nature and her lesbian friend, The Environment, a good turn.

Art in the vineyard

Vineyards cannot function at anywhere near optimum capacity unless they feature striking statues. Large metal statues are best, featuring legendary heroic figures; non-representational pieces, such as bits of scrap metal badly welded together and called 'Homecoming' or 'A Thunderstorm in Blue', have been shown in recent Icelandic research to encourage every grape disease, pest, and act of God conceivable. They should be treated with extreme caution.

Appropriate vineyard sculptures are guaranteed to improve cellar-door sales.

For the décor near the cave door, water features aren't a bad idea – and visitors tend to love seeing some sort of excavation. Any hole in the ground will do, preferably dug into the side of a hill. The visitors stand and gaze at it for hours, commenting in the most mind-numbing way about soil profiles, drainage, mineral deposits, and water retention. Anyone bothering to listen to them would think that soil was an important factor in establishing and maintaining a vineyard. What rot! That's what fertiliser is for.

Animals and pests

A vineyard must also have top-rate staff to work behind the counter in the cellar door, or cave. These young people operate the cash register and credit card machines when visitors buy wine. They also assist the visitor in tasting the wine that the vineyard either produces or buys in. Their role in this endeavour is to gently massage visitors' moronic comments about wine to the point where the visitor feels so empowered by their own wine tasting prowess that they buy cases of the stuff – and all at a healthy cellar door mark-up price too. My great mate Richard Branson, when he first set up his airline business, spent weeks working behind the counter at one of my wineries in Kent. He made no bones about the fact that he was there to learn the ropes, so to speak, of selling affordable aspiration. He has been kind enough to name more than one of his aircraft after my vineyards.

Dogs also help in the vineyard. Their principal role is to look friendly and wag their tails and woof amiably at any visitor to the cellar door. This happy barking, however, is no fluke of canine nature: the best vineyard dogs have been trained to sound such an alarm in order to warn the cellar-door staff that more victims are approaching. This gives the staff time to put out their cigarettes, turn off the football, and switch on the classical music. Certain breeds are better than others, but this is regionally specific. Indeed, dog breed regionality is one of the big issues our industry will have to face over the next century.

In Germany, any pointer will do – as long as it has one of those hairy snouts not dissimilar to Nietzsche's moustache. French dogs range from silly little lap dogs that probably derive from Belgium to more solid hunting dogs that have long ears and absolutely no work ethic. In Spain, all the dogs were killed in Franco's War; in Italy, the dogs are tourists from America. In California, the dogs are usually Samoyed, Rhodesian Ridgebacks, Newfoundlands or Portuguese Water Dogs. They are usually congenitally handicapped. In Australia, they have Cattle Dogs, which seem either permanently drunk or, at the very least, punch-drunk. They have names like Pinot, too. New Zealanders like Labradors or Border Collies or any breed that enjoys riding around in the back of a Volvo Estate.

Accessories

Top-rate vineyards will also have a balloon. The basket should ideally hold up to twelve people and the balloon itself should be emblazoned with your chateau's name. Get this aircraft out every time you entertain international media or supermarket-chain wine buyers. Have it float over the vineyard at no more than twelve feet above the vines and that ought to do the trick. While on the topic of military equipment in vineyards, a cannon or some other piece of ordinance never goes astray when impressing VIPs.

The vista, paraphernalia, and staff are all well and good, of course, but nowadays no jet-setting wine tourist worth their platinum credit card will take you seriously unless your winery/chateau/estate has a few stainless steel tanks, in which – apparently – one makes wine. Do not waste your money on these faddish pieces of nonsense. Instead, employ a *trompe-l'oeil* painter and have the side of your tractor shed transformed into the appropriate view. This is not only cheaper, but you can sleep restfully at night knowing that you have done the right thing by the local arts community. They, after all, will be the ones buying the bulk of your Vino Della Casa. A little bit of goodwill goes a long way in this business.

CHAPTER 5

Regions of the world

My very own journey through the wide, wonderful, moist world of wine.

I've been to paradise, but I've never been to me.
KOFI ANNAN,
SECRETARY GENERAL OF THE UNITED NATIONS

The rich kaleidoscope of the world's many and varied wine regions and districts is far too big a topic to cover in detail here. I would instead point my readers to my seminal work, *Oberon Kant's Crazy, Crazy World of Wine*, published in 1964 by my great mate Mitchell Beazley. This book revolutionised wine publishing and brought a new intellectual rigour to the almost lost art of viticultural cartography. However, as no book on wine would be complete without exquisite hand-drawn maps strewn with quaint regional place names, I have included here a small selection of my favourite wine regions.

ITALY

There are few more tranquil experiences in the world of wine than sitting in a *Gondola del Vino* as it casually punts across the still waters at dawn towards the famous floating vineyards of Lake Garda. Established as a joint venture between the Medicis and the Doge in 1520, these remarkable vineyards are planted in floating islands composed of vine clippings woven through vast mats of discarded grape stalks. Once owned by my great mate Sergio Bellasconi but now in the hands of the Versace family, these extraordinarily beautiful floating vineyards produce some of the finest wines and grappa Italy has to offer.

These islands are, however, in grave and mortal danger. While they have been known to drift in the past – often requiring teams of trained viticulturists to search for days on end to find them – the islands have recently gone missing for whole months at a time, which can severely upset flowering and delay ripening. The islands are also under threat of flooding from the wash created by the constant wake of speedboats piloted by over-zealous 'slow-food' activists claiming to be protecting the cultural heritage of the region. Ah, the misguided passion of idealism.

Established: 1520.
Principal grape varieties: Amarone and Vin Santo.
Principal vine diseases: caffeine.
Fashionability: in summer.
Kant Rating: ☠☠☠

Burgundy

My introduction to Burgundy in the early 1970s was a riotous affair. We had just finished lunch at my great mate Alain Ducasse's restaurant (the now-legendary Pied de Cochon) and were hurtling down the A40 towards Macon in Alain's 2CV, when a box of air-dried chicken kidneys fell from a passing delivery van and landed in my lap. Without blinking, Ducasse reached down under his seat, pulled out a bottle of old Aligote and ripped the cork from the bottle with his teeth. The rest of the journey passed by in a haze, but I seem to remember Depardieu and Delon committing unspeakable acts in the back seat and that we had to pull over at one point while Truffaut loaded more film into his camera. Ah, heady, heady days.

Established: 1123. **Re-established:** 1976.
Principal grape varieties: Burgundy (red and white).
Principal vine diseases: fraud.
Fashionability: far too high, I'm afraid.
Kant Rating: ☠☠☠☠

Far north-west Western Australia

Kimberley Creek Ridge Estate, far north-west Western Australia. Here we see the cellar door on a particularly busy day.

Australia is the greatest example of technology triumphing over nature. Here, in the once-parched wilderness of the driest nation on earth, man has ingeniously installed vast gleaming networks of stainless steel irrigation, hydroelectric dams and temperature-controlled fermentation dripper lines to bring life-giving water, acid adjustment and oenotannin to the desert, creating a verdant vineyard from the arid sand. Ever since, wine has been the civilising force in the development of the culture of the

Republic of Australia. Without wine, there would be no sponsorship of the opera, sport or horse racing, and the population of this island continent would still be swilling Fosters in outback roadhouses rather than sipping fine Riesling at harbourside restaurants, which in recent years, has become the national pastime.

Established: 1788.
Principal grape varieties: industrial.
Principal vine diseases: marketing.
Fashionability: far too high, I'm afraid.
Kant Rating: ☠☠

The equatorial vineyards of Columbia are the home of phylloxera. It was here in 1836 that the deadly vine predator first came to the attention of a team of student ampelographers holidaying in the rainforest. Local Mayan winemakers had kept the pest in check for centuries by beating the creatures with sticks – a technique that had the beneficial side effect of inducing stress-related yield reduction in the grapes. The students took a pair of particularly gregarious animals back to Montpellier for a party and they escaped somewhere near Dijon, quickly multiplying and eventually devastating the vineyards of Europe.

In an ironic twist of cruel fate, the Columbian vineyards are now home to the Bogotá campus of the University of California, and are used to train viticulturists and imprison swarthy-looking teenagers suspected of unlawful winemaking.

Established: 1496.
Principal grape varieties: poppies and coca leaves.
Principal vine diseases: the CIA.
Fashionability: high, especially in polite society.
Kant Rating: ☠

Madeira

Madeira is the largest of a group of volcanic island located in the Atlantic Ocean approximately 640 kilometres off the west coast of Africa. First settled by the Portuguese in the fifteenth century, the island soon become home to a tapestry of vines grown in arbours on steep terraces on the mountain slopes.

Madeira's main port, Funchal, soon became an important stopping place for American colonists. The high acid, sweet wine that the island produced was used as ballast on the colonists' ships after being fortified with brandy before a long voyage. By the time it reached America the wine had literally been cooked – a process which increased, rather than decreased, its quality. Madeira became incredibly fashionable in the colonies during the eighteenth century, prized for its extraordinary amalgam of smoky characters and exquisite balance between sweetness and rapier-sharp acidity. The best eighteenth century Madeira wines still drink wonderfully – the acidity acting as an immortal preservative.

Established: 1420.
Principal grape varieties: Madeira comes in four styles – Sercial (the driest); Verdelho (medium dry, slightly honeyed); Bual (sweet and smoky) and Malmsey (dark brown and richly sweet).
Principal vine diseases: fungal diseases.
Fashionability: low, which is a shame, as the quality is often very high.
Kant Rating: 🏆🏆🏆🏆🏆

Eastern Europe

Czech vineyards are planted in ordered rows.

I was recently taken on a tour of the art nouveau mineral springs of Eastern Europe – a small town just outside London. Here, smoked eel sausages and Pilsener beer are taken with every glass of wine. All wineries have a brewery on site – a leftover of this land's communist past, when cellars were state-owned and concrete fermentation tanks doubled as Stasi interrogation chambers (in vats, no-one can hear you scream). This idyllic setting was ruined by the Happy Shopper Corporation, particularly through their range of Wybrojzna Ridge Chardonnay – recommended by my great mates Lech and Vaclav, both of whom are directors of the company.

Established: 1990.
Principal grape varieties: crystal hops.
Principal vine diseases: democracy and MTV.
Fashionability: Prada.
Kant Rating: no stars, but a half sickle for effort.

CHAPTER 6

The art, craft and science of winemaking

Some of my great mates are winemakers – these are their stories.

The only thing I wear to bed is Chanel No. 5.
ROBERT PARKER JR

My great mate Brother John May, Jesuit winemaker at Sevenhill in Clare, South Australia once said to me, 'Oberon, wine is a gift from God. If you were to crush grapes and throw them into a barrel, the naturally occurring yeasts would transform the juice into wine.' Brother John is a man of God obviously familiar with many Algerian wines. 'The winemaker's job,' his constant refrain, 'is to give God a helping hand.' Ah so true.

Apart from wine writers, winemakers are the most important people alive on this planet today. Without them there would be no wine. Without wine there would be nothing to write about. Without wine journalism today's buyers wouldn't know what to drink.

My great mate and spiritual adviser, Brother John May.

Winemakers are heroic creatures who devote their entire lives to the divine vocation of winemaking. They are strong, passionate men (and women too, nowadays) who realise their life is to create pleasure for others. And for that, I thank them.

I would like to introduce you to some of the winemakers I have met in my vast travels.

Devon Van Dannon

When so many traditions are broken in the New World it's a wonder how these societies stay together. Many don't – you only have to ask my great mate Pik Van Der Bok how his vintage is going in the Cape and you can hear his heavy head shaking over the phone. In Australia – the country I chose to retire to after my doctor insisted that the clean antipodean air and sunshine would do wonders for my liver – broken traditions are a way of life.

A neighbour of mine – a young lad I see as somewhat of a protégé, although he's far too proud to admit it – makes wine in the most extraordinary way and is one

Devon Van Dannon came from a long line of master blasters.

of three winemakers currently under surveillance by ASIO, the local secret police.

When I say that he is a neighbour, this is of course, simply relative. He lives and works in Loxton, a wine ghetto some 1500 kilometres downstream from my sheep station on the Murray River. But in this brown, wine land, sorry, brown, wide land (or is that wide, brown land? – I always forget), thousands of kilometres cannot separate like-minds, so he is a neighbour of sorts.

To many Europeans, for whom winemaking is an art passed down from father to bastard son, Van

Dannon's method of cultivation, harvesting and winemaking seems odd – he uses high explosives. The sun-stroked locals, however, find the practice a somewhat quaint (if a little noisy and lethal) form of making a living from the land.

His father, Rutger Van Dannon, was an outback water diviner. With two strips of copper in his hands, Rutger would wander the red soil of northern South Australia and start convulsing in an obscene manner whenever he passed over bodies of subterranean water. He'd mark the site with his boots, spend the evening preparing explosives and reading from the bible, then wake up the next morning before dawn and blow a great hole in the ground. After receiving payment from the station owner, he would return to the Clare Valley on his chestnut mare where he would court the lovely Maggie Schitthe – his future wife and sister of (the late) Leo Schitthe.

Rutger eventually married Maggie one afternoon in autumn at the Tanunda town hall. It is rumoured that their first son, Devon, was conceived that night on a sack of detonators in a nearby explosives warehouse.

Devon, like his father, roamed the district blowing holes in the earth. He soon settled in Cessnock in New South Wales' Hunter Valley where his zest for explosives and love of good wine came together when clearing a block of scrub for Murray Tyrrell. With a small amount of TNT placed in a gentle fold of the well-worn earth, he carefully managed to fell 30 solid acres of eucalypts and permanently deafen a herd of Tyrrell's prize Angus with one well-thought-out blast.

The meagre earnings from this day's work were enough for Van Dannon to buy a small plot of land in the semi-arid lower reaches of the Murray River. With the eye of an eagle, the heart of a master winemaker and bravado that would later enthral the author of the *Guns of Navarone*, Devon Van Dannon tied twenty tonnes of high explosives to a small wooden tower and blasted out 300 acres of useless Mallee, thereby ensuring himself a place in the history books and the files of Australia's internal security organisation.

'There's no landscape on earth I can't grow grapes in' is Devon's catchcry. If the earth is too stony, he bores out a matrix of small holes, fills each with a stick of gelignite, lays out the wiring, then detonates. As soon as the dust has settled, a team of fencers and irrigators pick their way through the stunned wildlife and local residents and set up the trellises and drip lines. A week later, the vine stock goes in. 'You never need to worry about fertility,' says Van Dannon, 'there's enough ammonium nitrate left over for a thousand vintages.'

To many winemakers, a flat, arid plain is seen as useless ground – but not Van Dannon. With TNT and a good crosswind he can turn dull limestone country into a Tolkien-esque fairy wonderland. 'In any deep crater there's bound to be at least 90 north-facing degrees', he says licking the dust from his lips. 'Tri-Nitro-Toluene is the best growth stimulant there is!'

After learning how to make terroir from explosives, Van Dannon set about using 'rapidly expanding chemical reactions' (his words not mine) in every facet of the winemaking process. When pruning, for example, a small hand grenade is lobbed into a luxuriant mass of dead vines to dislodge all but the hardiest, most tenacious canes.

Instead of buying expensive mechanical harvesters, Van Dannon will let off a small rocket in his vineyards. The force from the afterburners knock the ripest grapes to the ground, leaving smaller, less ripe fruit to be harvested a week later with a series of surface-to-air missiles.

In some wineries, crushing is still done by presses. Van Dannon sees the way of the future being shaped by limpet mines detonated above the grapes, rupturing the fruit, allowing little contact with the skin – perfect for the delicate Riesling Van Dannon makes so well.

Many would say Van Dannon is a heretic, I say he's a saint. His method of clarifying wines stops the need for any animal products such as isinglass, albumen or fuller's earth. To settle his wines at Murray Flat Hills, Van Dannon uses a small explosive taped to each barrel, which is detonated at the beginning of each month. The sulphur that is forced into the barrels is seen by some lesser-educated critics as a flaw. I see the breathtaking qualities of his sulphur-rich wines as an ineffable yardstick.

When bottling, Devon Van Dannon doesn't just snub his nose at the traditional Champagne makers in Epernay – he completely blows it off. Added sugar may give bubbles to some *méthode champenois* but to Van Dannon there's nothing better than a good vial of nitro-glycerine. A few drops added to every bottle after disgorgement adds billions of fine bubbles – and a small flash after the cork is popped.

Although a slightly taciturn gentleman (Van Dannon has been known to sit in silence rocking back and forth for days at a time), he is comparatively gregarious when it comes time to release his wine. In the centre of a large cathedral-like room he has built from the tors and obelisks he has wrenched from the earth, a bonfire rages. Gently, he places a small bugle to his lips, and as each wine is carried in on a gilded tray he plays one slightly off-key note. At that moment, using a remote-control device hidden in his other hand, he sets off a rather large amount of TNT perched on an island in one of the many irrigation dams at Murray Flat Hills. Although no food and very little wine is served at these launches he always manages to get scores of press people, a few wine writers and bus loads of current affairs and news journalists.

Devon Van Dannon does not, in fact, produce very

much wine at all. From his 1000 or so acres under vine, he makes about 100 cases. His intensive explosives program allows very few grapes to actually set, let alone ripen. Most vines bear shrapnel wounds – some only produce one good cane. Because of his low yield and heavy use of high explosives, Van Dannon is able to charge prices now approaching US$2500 per bottle.

Sister Wilhelmina Gotha

I first met Sister Wilhelmina soon after the war. Germany was a weak and fairly messy nation, still cowering after the humiliating defeat. The Germans hung their heads low as they roamed their still-smouldering cities.

As an attaché to the American army, I was given carte blanche to scour the countryside investigating vulnerable companies who may have been able to benefit from the assistance of the Marshall Plan. (Some may say we were aggressive carpet-baggers taking over foreign companies at gunpoint – but it was essential to the nation's reformation. It is a little known fact that I was instrumental in rebuilding the German wine industry with postwar American dollars.)

It was a warm autumnal September evening. I remember it well because the local *swinemeisters* were feeding acorns to their hogs. While my American guides – Lieutenant Grobowski and his team – were defusing mines on the Schloss Käse Bridge in the Mosel (an operation during which one of his men lost an ear while listening for explosive devices) I wandered into a nearby vineyard. While admiring the laden vines pregnant with fruit, I leant down to fondle a large bunch of green and yellow grapes. I felt a presence behind me – then a sharp blow delivered to the back of my skull. As I was losing consciousness, I made out a black-hooded figure towering over me holding the butt of a gun in her hand.

I came to three days later in a brightly lit room overlooking the Weisse Zweibeln Fluss (White Onion River). Above the gentle sound of water lapping on rocks I could hear the shrill sound of squealing pigs and laughing women. Under my bed sheets, I could feel I had been dressed in a silk shroud. Suddenly, a young nun entered the room carrying a pewter jug and a tray of what appeared to be black pudding. She spoke perfect English: 'You will have been sleeping here Herr, you Kant,' she said, to which I replied 'Why not? '

She poked a strand of blonde hair under her wimple and wafted a sausage under my nose. 'You must eat and drink to recover your strength. Sister Gotha is awaiting you.' The young nun, Sister Dürer, then poured me a mug of thick beer. It tasted strongly of barley with very little acid balance. 'I see you are displeased with the bier,' she said. 'We are expecting hops from our sister order in Belgium next month. The war has changed many things.'

And so it had. The Abbey of Saint Hilda in Mosel was once a place of higher learning. Before the war, it had taken a lot of young English girls denounced by their upper-class families for all manner of abnormalities. Many of the girls were born out of wedlock, others were slightly too tall to marry and one young lass had an unappealing lisp. During the war, St Hilda's had become a self-sufficient commune supplying all manner of smallgoods to the nearby POW camp.

St Hilda's was run by a young nun, Sister Wilhelmina Gotha. I later learnt that she was born to a powerful English family in their castle in Berkshire but could not claim her family's name because her father was king and her mother an American divorcee.

The young Sister Dürer spoon-fed me the superb *assiette* of Teutonic *charcuteries*. 'Eat up – the flesh is made stronger by eating the flesh of another beast', she said.

Later that day I was helped out of the silk shroud – a garment I still sleep in to this day – and led through dark cloisters to a small, walled garden. I reeled around to see the same black figure that had pistol-whipped me three days earlier.

'I'm sorry about the inconvenience', came the mellifluous voice. The figure pulled back her hood to reveal a cascade of flaming red hair. 'But we have to be so careful these days', she continued. Her face was freckled from summers under the harsh German sun. Her lips were pursed like a newly opened rosebud. Her nose was strongly familiar – broad yet defined: capable of placing itself over the rim of a tasting glass, I thought to myself.

'There has been so much evil in this time', she continued. With that she snapped a vine cleanly between two fingers and placed the limb in a basket hanging over her arm. This was Sister Gotha. 'You are a man of infinite taste and honest wisdom', I think I recall her saying. 'I can see in you what I have been searching for', she said as she led me through the vineyard.

A devoutly Christian woman, she had stopped planting her new vines in customary rows. Instead she instructed her nuns to plant her vineyards in the shape of crucifixes. Criss-crossing that great hill at Mosel were great crosses of vines. White varieties marked the cross; red varieties formed the body of Christ.

'Kneel!' she suddenly screamed as we approached the centre of one planting, 'and feel the power of the

Lord.' She grabbed my head and thrust it into a ripe bunch of red grapes. Her powerful arms and hands pushed my face into the ripe, red berries; the skin of bursting grapes clung to my chin. Juice ran down my chest, onto my mesh vest and down my stomach. Overwhelmed by carnal sensations, fettled and confused by an extensive and expensive education, I once again collapsed.

Two days later, after regaining consciousness, I was asked by Sister Gotha to supervise the vintage. As I followed her down to the vineyard, I caught a glimpse of Sister Dürer throwing dry wood onto a great pyre on the other side of the cloisters. It was nearly three metres high topped by what looked like a chair. It reminded me of those great bonfires the pagan club in Kensington used to put on each year.

Out on the hills, the nuns were harvesting furiously – chanting as they went. This was long before the days of mechanical harvesting and every person was needed to bring in the crop. Sister Gotha was no exception. She leant across the grape vines and started shaking. Her freckled face turned deep violet as her hips shot back and forth, pounding the vines with pressure from the lower, vastly more powerful half of her body. The grapes fell into the waiting cloths. Only the fullest, ripest grapes fell. She repeated the manoeuvre row after cross-like row. The juice-laden fruit was then carefully dropped into carved bowls and taken to a stern but ailing mother superior (I remember her having only one good eye – the other glazed over like a custard-covered marble). She supervised the crushing, which was carried out not by foot but by the entire bodies of the nuns, who threw themselves onto the grapes and screamed in German to let the spirit of the Lord enter them. The sight was both appalling and, in an intellectual way, quite endearing. Later, Sister Gotha asked me to change into my white silk shroud as we were going into a sterile area to inoculate the grape juice with yeast. This she did while chanting an ancient liturgy in what sounded not dissimilar to Aramaic. Her voice was so soothing and encouraging that I did not notice I was being led up a ladder to the top of the pyre. Just as Sister Dürer was placing my wrists into the calf leather straps, there was a toot from the horn of Lieutenant Grobowski's Jeep. Shaken out of my strange fug, I looked Sister Dürer in the eye and smiled at her. She was in a trance-like state, not seeing me but seeing what I know not what. I slid down the ladder and departed, leaving a ring of nuns wielding fiery torches.

Half a decade later I finally tasted the wine produced by Sister Gotha. Although undrinkable, the almost sugar-like qualities of that vintage led me to recommend the style to a famous German winemaker who created a wine reminiscent of the purple-blue colour she betook during the harvest of her grapes. I will always lament the Blue Nun.

Jethro Dawe

It is widely claimed by many that the British Isles underwent a mild period of climatic change during the twelfth century. It is alleged that a southern swell in the Gulf Stream bathed England in a short but glorious period of warm weather. For 50 years grapes from Normandy were planted in Hampshire and Kent and Old Blighty was blessed with wine of her own.

English winemakers thrived. Londoners moved away from drinking ale to enjoy what became known as Vin de Surrey. But there were victims. Mead makers were

Jethro would occasionally resort to village girls after exhausting his supply of backpackers.

unable to sell their liquor, so they were forced to abandon their hives. For decades, parts of England were inundated with swarms of feral bees. The other victims were the traditional fruit and vegetable winemakers. These were men who didn't need grapes to make wine. To them, anything with sugar in it could be fermented into alcohol: carrot, parsnip, plum – even hedgehogs. 'If it grew, it will brew', they used to say.

Despite this appalling cultural decimation, a small handful of winemakers survived to pass knowledge down through the centuries. A precious few still make Vin de Vegetable in the quaint old West Country manner today.

One of them is a willowy chap from Cornwall named Jethro Dawe. Last time I saw him, Baroness Thatcher was at the height of her powers and, despite being told that 'God was looking over that green and pleasant land', everything did not seem in its place. The train had passed through Teignmouth and I was travelling towards the nearby village of Quimmerby, lurching around the tight little corners of the country railway. As we rounded a particularly long corner, from my seat next to the driver I could see smoke rising from a hundred small fires. It looked like a scene from a Brueghel – only with great yellow bulldozers instead of horse carts. The ancient hedgerows of Britannia were being ripped from the earth and heaped into piles. Small men in EU-approved safety vests were setting them alight. Homeless songbirds hovered overhead, unable to find a roost. Badgers and foxes – formerly natural enemies – ran side-by-side fleeing the carnage in search of refuge. I was quite unnerved.

The train lurched to a stop at Quimmerby station. Two old men with ruddy cheeks sat on a hay bale outside the post office. I asked them where I could find Jethro Dawe. One replied, 'That'll be Jethro's son Jethro you're lookin' for', with that quaint, but rather annoying Cornish drawl.

The other old fool shook his head. 'You've missed him', he said, his hands resting on a walking stick. 'He'll have been gone for a while now', he said.

'Gone?' I said. 'Jethro Dawe, the finest winemaker in Cornwall, gone?'

'That's right,' came the reply, 'there wasn't a vegetable in the west he couldn't turn into wine. The vicar toasted my wife and me on our wedding day with a pint of his Turnip Champagne.'

'I think you'll find it was Cabbage Sherry', corrected his friend.

'So where has he gone?' I demanded, barely stifling a frustrated scream.

'Just down the road, past the vicar's house', said the old grey bearded man. 'Left at the vestry, third grave on the right.'

'He went last October while he was pickin' brambles', continued the other. 'He was getting on in years and was wearing a pair of those fleece-lined slippers. Made them himself he did. Silly old bugger forgot to wash 'em – they was covered with the scent of a ewe. A ewe in heat. His old ram took a shining to those slippers, again and again. Coroner said "Death By Misadventure", but Misadventure were a funny name for a Poll Dorset ram.'

I turned away defeated, thinking about my poor Devon winemaker, resting in peace under a yew tree after what must have been a horrendous end. As I headed back to the station, one of the village idiots called out: 'But you might want to pay a visit to Jethro's young son, Jethro. He's expecting you.'

The main drive to Oak Puck Farm was soft under foot. Instead of the usual crushed rock, the surface was made up entirely of kernels of stone fruit, apple pips and the dried-out tops of old root vegetables.

'Orright there sir', came a voice from high up in a mulberry tree. A thin man with a satchel over his shoulder shinnied down the tree like a monkey. He extended a large gnarled hand and introduced himself.

'Jethro Dawe. I is pleased to meet you,' he said from a scar of a mouth set into a long drawn out face with ruddy cheeks, punctuated by a nose with broken capillaries. He wore a straw hat, yeoman's smock and

Nike trainers. I felt assured that there was at least some part of the West Country that Thomas Hardy could still recognise.

He led me past his dovecote, ducks and guinea fowl to a barn made of stone with a thatched roof. Inside were great baskets brimming with fruit and vegetables. In one corner stood a massive press, its immense crushing power coming from a well-worn block of stone. A rope led from a spike in the stone through a pulley and then outside where it was connected to a leather harness. It was the last remaining donkey-powered vegetable press in England and, unfortunately, Jethro's donkey was lame.

Resourceful as all country people are, he had enlisted the help of two Scandinavian backpackers, who were strapped up in the donkey harness.

With a small yell and a flick of a whip, Jethro ordered the backpackers to pull the stone weight. Bleating and frothing at the mouth in a manner that would have attracted the attention of RSPCA wardens in any civilised county, the backpackers lurched forward and the stone rose high up above the press. Jethro tied the press down, released the rope from the hapless backpackers, threw in a basket of swedes and mangel-wurzels, then pulled on an old wooden lever. The stone came down with a sickening thud and from the bottom of the press came a stream of golden juice that frothed up in a wooden pail. Jethro picked up the pail and hurled it into a yawning oak vat. This process was repeated until the backpackers lay exhausted in the mud outside and the vat was half full of pungent liquid.

'That'll be it there until the stench of fermenting juice drives the owls out the barn', said Jethro lazily. 'That's when I know it's ready for bottlin',' he continued.

Later, over a meal in his cottage with his wife (who bore an eerie familial resemblance to her spouse) Jethro opened a bottle, its label obscured by one of his oafish hands. He had previously retrieved it from his cellar – more converted pigsty than underground facility. In it lay untold and unmarked vintages of the West Country's finest. His Asparagus and Bramley Cox Pippin Apple Champagne was reminiscent of a cold climate sparkling Chardonnay. Jethro's Blackberry and Rhubarb could easily be mistaken for a Burgundy blended with a young Verdelho. One of his more intriguing blends was a Parsley and Mustard wine that reminded me of bad Shiraz in which was steeped a washed rind cheese. Somehow though, despite the sheer assault of these wines, I rapidly became very fond of them.

Jethro lifted the bottle he had been uncorking and poured a dark red liquid that clung to the glass like date syrup. It was concurrently gamy, smokey and earthy. I racked my brain trying to detect the flavours. With the two recovered backpackers looking on – safely on the other side of the kitchen window – I sniffed and savoured and swished but could not for the dear life of me figure how he had made such an interesting wine that had such complex structure underwritten with strong faecal and putrescent notes.

'Jethro my good man,' I said in desperation, 'what varieties of vegetables did you use to make this extraordinary wine?'

'Those weren't no ordinary vegetable,' he said rather sheepishly, 'those were once animals.' I was dumbfounded. He explained that the game flavours came from a triple-crushed haunch of venison, the smokiness from a late-picked Finan Haddock. 'And,' he continued 'there's just a few hedgehogs in there to give it a nice earthy structure to balance.'

As I wandered back to the train station I became aware of a scurrying mass of creatures heading towards Oak Puck Farm. Among the acres of rambling carrot patches, parsnip hedges and mangel-wurzel plantations, the faunal refugees were fleeing the bulldozing on the surrounding farms for the relative safety of Oak Puck Farm. There, the badgers could frolic in the rambling carrot patches, the otters could swim under the quince trees and the foxes make lairs in the parsnip patches – until Jethro's next vintage.

Pedro 'El Diablo' Escovar

It is said that when Pedro Escovar walked into a room, women could sense a change in humidity. Chile's greatest winemaker had a smile and presence that could charm women, men, animals and plants alike. Standing six-foot two-inches tall, tresses of long black hair falling over broad shoulders, he was a man with angular features that supported a smile that was both wicked and boyish. His grip was warm and welcoming, finishing with a clench that left you in no doubt that he was not a man to be crossed. A keen horseman and a lover of other men's wives, he was the maker of wine that, as local legend has it, made the weak strong and the strong euphoric. It is little wonder then that although Pablo Escovar was lauded as a national hero he was secretly referred to under every Chilean's breath as 'El Diablo' – the devil.

The ever-charming Pedro 'El Diablo' Escovar.

Pedro was born in Spain sometime in the nineteenth century. The exact time and place of his birth are pure speculation but it is reported by some that he suffered his own personal inquisition at the age of nineteen after a young contessa succumbed to his irresistible charm. Fleeing the prospect of a duel with the contessa's brother, he left his homeland behind him – along with the name 'El Cajhones Magnifico' – and boarded a ship bound for California. With a bundle of cuttings smuggled under his vest, he hoped to make his fortune growing Sherry grapes for the wealthy Forty-Niners.

A freak storm dashed his ship upon a reef in Tierra del Feugo. Washed upon a rocky shore, legend has it that he made a pact with Satan himself, who came to him in the guise of a sea elephant, exchanging powerful winemaking skills for Escovar's soul.

For three months Escovar travelled north, heeling the stolen cuttings into the dry, cold ground as he went. These vines somehow prospered and naturally hybridised with native Andean psychotropic medicinal plants. It is uttered that, in later years, he would return to these new cross-bred vines and take further cuttings to provide nematode-resistant root stock for his Bordeaux clones. Of course, this is all South American superstitious nonsense, but it does give weight to the fact that he became the best New World winemaker of his day without a skerrick of knowledge in the great art of winemaking.

So in this remote, sun-blessed yet snow-chilled nation where democracy simply means that every citizen has the right to be thrown out of a plane if they merely complain about a parking ticket, Escovar thrived like his mythical hybrids.

As an example, I repeat the story once told to me by one of his dismissed cellarmasters. Apparently, one night while gambling with the Duke of Northumbria in the port town of Valparaiso, he won a small parcel of barren land near San Felipe. Later, standing on a rocky outcrop of his holdings with the cold evening air flowing down from the Andes, he raised his palms to the sky. The ground shook, the sky erupted into fire and llamas bellowed like bulls. It was an earthquake of biblical proportions. The next day the local Indians peered out from their neighbouring *pueblos* to see Pedro's rock-strewn farm covered in fine soil. That morning, he was named 'Diablo del Terroir', later shortened to 'El Diablo'.

But Escovar's tale was far from finished. Neighbouring vineyards were inexplicably stricken with locusts, phylloxera and spontaneous cellar-door infernos. As they closed, Pedro simply bought them up one by one. On his frequent trips to Santiago, he made love to many women – including the wife of the future president Salvador Allende. (It is often said that Allende's daughter, Isabella, owes her mysterious storytelling powers to the man who sold his soul to a blubbery sea mammal.)

The devil incarnate?

It was the late 1960s when I first met Pedro 'El Diablo' Escovar. Although an old man, he still had much of the charm and malicious power I had read about years earlier in *Boy's Own Wine Hero* annuals. He was slightly stooped but still had the flashing smile – albeit flashed from the teeth pulled from a poor Andean boy. His mane of shoulder length hair was still black, although it did reek of shoe polish. Extending the legendary palms that once turned rock into soil, he took my hands into his in a gesture that both welcomed and terrified me. 'Welcome to Casa de Escovar', he said. He clicked his fingers and one of his many daughters came forth with a bottle of old vine Carmenere and three glasses. 'So kind Señor,' I said, 'but there are only two of us yet we have three glasses.'

His eyes darkened. 'That is because we drink to another who you cannot see.' With that, he poured the glass of blood-red Carmenere that clung to the glass with butterfly wings that seemed to edge up to the lip of the stemware as if they were trying to escape. He raised both glasses in his hands to a west-facing window, bowed his head sightly and proceeded to drink from both. 'Sante', he whispered hoarsely. I toasted his unseen fenestral familiar and then tapped the glass and placed it to my ear, as I always do. What I heard in that glass was not the singing of peasants or the sound of panpipes so familiar in Chilean wines, but the sad roar of the Antarctic Ocean and the distant wallowing of walruses. This was a wine made from his legendary Tierra del Feugo vines grown in his Aconcaguan vineyard. Its perfume was heady – all berries, sun and mountain water diverted from the melting snow to irrigate his vineyard. The flavour was exceptional and the effect bedazzling. Moments of conquistadors flashed before me: gold-covered mountains and fleeing Indians; blood and earthquakes; mountain pumas and Mayan cities. I found myself floating above the peaks of the Andes, before zooming above the deserts of northern Chile. The experience was unusual but not unique. (I had a similar vision in Mexico after a Mescal and single malt tasting with my mate Bevan Bevis – the award-winning whisky journalist. After that night there are three solid weeks of my life that I cannot account for, but somehow I was elected governor of Chihuahua.)

Escovar was grinning at me. 'This, my friend, is what I call "Mi Amigo Negro",' he said, 'or how you say in English? "My Black Chum" perhaps?'

His evil smile prevented me from correcting his awkward, if not patronising, attempt at translation. His 'Black Friend', however, was a seductive red wine that could not be bought for money. Wealthy families would instead offer their youngest son as an indentured worker in exchange for one case of Black Friend to be delivered by a secretive lone donkey each year on Shrove Tuesday, between 7 p.m. and ten past.

As to the current whereabouts of Pedro 'El Diablo' Escovar, no one is quite sure. He left his vineyards one day after pruning his small corner of Malbec by charming the fruitless cordons off the vine. He then sailed off to Spain from Valparaiso in his yacht. Weeks later it was found drifting in a still patch of water to the north of Bermuda, the entire yacht intact – not unlike the *Mary Celeste.* A half-eaten omelette – still warm – was sitting on the galley table. Next to the plate was a bottle of Mi Amigo Negro and two nearly empty glasses – rivulets of wine still making their way back down to the sediment at the bottom. Despite all his faults, Escovar always kept his end of a bargain.

Autographs

Chapter 7

Buying wine

Negotiating the minefield that is purchasing one's weekly supplies; or why one needs to sleep with one's wine merchant on a regular basis.

Don't pay the ferryman, don't even fix the price.
Don't pay the ferryman, until he gets you to the other side.
Lady Catherine de Burgh, *Pride and Prejudice*

Buying wine is, apparently, a dangerous activity fraught with peril and danger. I seldom need to pay for wine myself, but my friends and acquaintances who are not lucky enough to have a steady supply generously donated to them by winemakers desperate for a kind word in one of my columns in the world's leading newspapers and magazines, tell me that it is imperative not to get too drunk at the many tastings that are, I believe, frequently held in the more progressive wine merchants' premises. My chums relate horrific tales of waking up the next morning in the back seat of the Bentley with a case of undrinkable Argentine

Malbec shoved under one's arm, having been shunted home along the tram tracks by some obliging young tram driver.

To avoid such embarrassment in the future, I here offer some tips for the wine buyer, drawing on my years of experience as consultant to the Harrods wine department and my intimate friendship with some of the world's leading wine merchants.

As a general rule it is vitally important to remember the three essential stages of buying wine. Once you have chosen your bottle and taken it to the counter, it is crucial that you hand over your credit card BEFORE walking out of the shop with your purchase. Yes, yes, I know this seems like such a trifling detail but I have it on good authority that to forget the middle stage of the transaction could lead to one being hauled in front of a magistrate – a ruddy-faced chap in his mid fifties with thick-set eyes and a manner that reminded me of a warthog on heat, although I managed to have the three week sentence suspended, thanks to my impeccable record.

Also, I suggest you only ever buy wine on Mondays, so as to avoid crowds.

Retailers

You can tell a great wine merchant as soon as you walk into the establishment. The floor will be spotless; the bottles carefully dusted and polished. Light classical music – Gluck, Chopin, Clayderman, et al. – will be warbling unobtrusively from cleverly concealed speakers. The staff will be well-groomed, have clean fingernails and polished shoes, wear neck ties, speak proper English, and will not be sporting such disgusting modern trappings as name tags, body piercings, tattoos, moustaches or breasts. Such a scenario, however, is all too rare. The era of the great wine merchant is all but passed.

Specialist Retailers

The best Burgundy specialist in the world, 'D'Or to Door', is based in Edinburgh and is operated with flair and individuality by my great mate Alexandre de Cante, the *Comte de Kant* (he hails from the French side of the family). Their wine lists are legendary among the trade – hand-engraved and printed on vellum by a family of crofters in the Outer Hebrides, these remarkable documents often reach higher prices at auction than the wines themselves.

Supermarkets

Indeed.

Buying from the Chateau

It is impossible to buy wine direct from the wine producer. Wine people are generous types in my extensive experience: regardless of where I happen to be in France, whenever I pull the Bentley into the car park of the local domaine or chateau, the *chef du cave* or the proprietor will always run out and throw case after case of both current and museum-release wines into the boot. It never ceases to amaze me how these people always seem to know who one is.

Direct Mail

This loathsome practice is, I believe, growing in popularity among the barbarous nations of the world, and in my opinion constitutes the worst invasion of privacy an Englishman can suffer. As my great mate Baroness Thatcher used to say when she was at

I have my Madeira flown in daily from Funchal.

the helm of the greatest empire on Earth: 'there is no such thing as a Wine Society – only individual wine merchants'. And how right she is.

Auctions

The great mistake many young wine aficionados make – and I have seen it done time and time again – is to be scrupulously honest when approaching the wine auction market. When you are describing the wines you need to sell, avoid terms such as 'flood-damaged label', 'level low shoulder' and 'weeping cork'. Instead, always use phrases such as 'mint condition', 'in original timber box' and 'signed by the winemaker'. By the time some fool stockbroker with his temperature-controlled walk-in cellar built into his inner-city warehouse-converted apartment gets his auction purchases delivered, you'll have left the country anyway.

Black Market

This is the way one buys wine in America. One is driven blindfolded to the local speakeasy (a quaint American term for a fine wine store) where one knocks on the door and asks for Tony. One is immediately shuffled inside where, in the gloom, one can make out shadowy figures and very attractive, spot-lit young sales assistants holding onto rather slippery poles. A bottle of Champagne appears on one's table, and one is instructed to drink. No money visibly changes hands and yet, by the end of the evening, one is considerably poorer. The American Government imposes strict controls on interstate wine shipping – a situation that has not changed since prohibition in the early 1970s. I well remember many years ago running a dozen magnums of 1945 Mouton into New York by hiding them inside Louis Armstrong's cheeks.

A great wine retailer.

Pre-Loved Wine

A great way of stocking one's cellar is to get one's staff to scour the classifieds for notices of deceased estates, impounded wine and customs fire sales. In these days of increased corporatisation in the wine industry internationally, I wouldn't be surprised to see half-page advertisements in the *Herald Tribune* or *Newsweek* for large quantities of very reasonable ex-demonstration or army surplus wine. As always, however, buyer-beware.

Online

I can wholeheartedly recommend the extraordinary wine website *Spittoon* (www.spittoon.com.au). Although I have a passing connection with the website (I own a 75 per cent stake and enjoy a generous consultant's fee linked directly to online sales) I feel I can be nonetheless totally objective and beyond reproach, and feel honour- and duty-bound to inform my readers about how *Spittoon* (www.spittoon.com.au) has had a profound effect on the wine world. Indeed, some commentators point out that it has changed forever the way we buy wine, and I can only agree. For more details, visit

www.Spittoon.com.au

Probably the best wine and food website in the world.

Tasting notes

Chapter 8

Reading the label

Cutting through the utter nonsense one encounters on modern wine labels like a knife through tepid lard.

'For what is the use of a book,' thought Alice, 'without pictures or conversations?'
Alice Cooper,
overheard by the (late) Queen Mother

here was a time when wine was sold in glass bottles without labels or tags – just a beautifully naked glass vessel filled to the neck with wine, leaving just enough room for a hand-whittled cork to be forcefully rammed into the opening. One didn't need to be told what was in the bottle. One simply, and quite naturally, knew. One only had to tap the bottle with a fish fork, place one's ear to the glass and listen for the delicate ringing that would tell one so much more than a thousand wine labels ever could.

Today such vessels, these *bouteilles nu*, are almost disparagingly called clean skins – as if there were something shameful about not being covered. This is because today's drinker has lost the skill to make up his (or her) own opinion about wine. This has left the public vulnerable to a deplorable team of persons responsible for polluting – even desecrating – the exterior of bottles with nonsensical words printed on layers of obscenely coloured paper or, even worse, plastic. (Here I must draw my breath, dear reader, to steady my nerves.)

Wine labels, I'm afraid, are here to stay. Having said that, I must add that there have been some exceptional pieces of art produced especially for labels. Being a well-respected painter myself, I have to admit that some of the chaps, Pablo, Salvador and Walt really did do some great works for the Rothschilds, but a wine bottle is no place to hold an art exhibition – that's why we have galleries and lap-top-dancing clubs. No, the art is on the other side of the glass – surrounded by it, waiting to be released to reach its full potential.

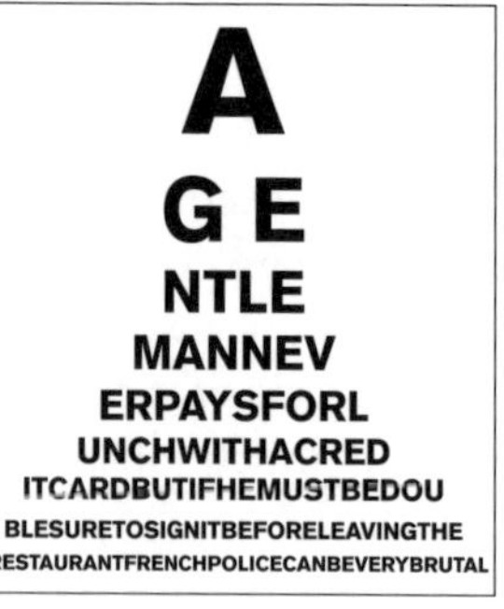

A wine label.

Following is a brief guide written to help the reader wade through the jargon without treating them like a child. So put down your pens, sit up straight and pay attention.

Front of Bottle

Take the nearest bottle and hold it in your hands. There may be one (perhaps two) paper squares, rectangles or diamonds on the bottle. These are labels. Go to the largest one. This is the front label. The word 'wine' generally indicates the bottle contains wine. The word 'wine' preceded by the words 'red' or 'white' generally indicates that the bottle contains either red or white wine. The word 'wine' succeeded by the word 'vinegar' indicates the contents may be a touch acidic for the general public. The term 'brewed alcoholic beverage made from grape concentrate' on the label means that the bottle you are about to consume was produced in an industrial estate somewhere in Arkansas.

Measure

Look at the bottom of the label and you will find some numbers followed by some letters, typically 750 ml, 75 cl or 27 fl oz. These are not dates in early Roman history. This is how much wine is in the bottle.

Alcohol

Nearby you will see a figure between five to around fifteen followed by the term ALC./VOL. The higher the number means the more alcohol in the wine. Multiply this number by the number of empty bottles sitting in front of you after a meal. If the final figure is less than 30 then it is perfectly safe to drive your 1972 orange Volvo Estate home.

Produce of . . .

The term 'Produce of ...' means that the wine was made in a country somewhere, and not on a converted fishing trawler twelve miles offshore in international waters.

Additives

There is an international system of numbered codes for identifying additives. Look for these carefully as they are indications of quality. If you find a wine label with any numbers around the 220s printed on the label then you know you are in possession of a Fine Wine. The more numbers the better. This means that the winemaker has invested much time and effort in adding all sorts of wonderful sulphurous additives and preservatives to give the wine a wonderfully breathtaking quality. If you see the number 621 on the bottle it means the wine was made with Chinese food in mind.

Back label

Reluctantly I have included a small section dedicated to the back label. The term itself is simply absurd and should be given absolutely no attention whatsoever under any circumstances. As wine bottles are perfectly cylindrical there is, by definition, no front or back.

In my opinion, the back label is simply a 200-word farrago of confusing terms and words designed to

make the prospective wine buyer hold the bottle just long enough to facilitate ownership of the bottle.

My great mate Peter Keeglehole from UCLA's massive wine department recently introduced me to some new software being developed in association with a company called Microvin. They have produced a programme called e-vin that can spit out a back label within three nanoseconds.

The programme isolates descriptors in seven categories. By printing out 2.2 randomly generated descriptors in gold ink on a red label, his e-vin programme can increase sales of very bland, ready-to-drink wine sixfold.

Listed below are the seven definite categories e-vin uses along with examples taken from the real world. They have been slightly modified for legal reasons. I have added my own no-nonsense explanations.

1. Parentage

'The late great Leo Schitthe first planted Shiraz grapes in the Butfolk Valley in the early 1850s'. This generally reflects a pathetic attempt by large wine companies to import some heritage value to their range of wines. It disguises the fact they were bought out by a large Dutch brewer only last Wednesday.

2. Non Pareil

'This wine is better than the wine from the winery next door because it is better'. This is generally an appalling misuse of axiom. Self-evident truth is only true when the end result is worth drinking. An obscene example of an advertising degree used for evil instead of good.

3. Manufacture

'This wine underwent maturation in oak hogsheads for eighteen months'. I find this sort of information appalling. It is tantamount to discussing how babies are made. This sort of language is best left to middle-class dinner parties.

4. Endorsement

'Barbra Streisand loves this wine'. Aha! Now some clear information the consumer can trust.

5. Target end use

'This wine is great with friends, while watching the sun set off the end of the pier'. This should read 'good seagull-repellent'.

6. Attribution

'This wine is better than others because it tastes like blackcurrant, cherries and smoke'. I think the best way to find out a wine's attributes is to fight alongside it in battle.

7. TARGET END USE MATCHING
'This wine is good with veal'. The wine has no flavour.

THE BIG BLACK COQ

2001

a Chianti style wine

13.5%alc.vol PRODUCE OF AUSTRALIA 750ml

A Fine Wine label – indeed a Very Fine Wine. Available now through all good retailers or visit

www.Spittoon.com.au

for details of your local stockist.

Symbols

In this post-literate age, many wine label designers and browsers are unable to read. Instead they use symbols to communicate. The following common symbols are thusly explained.

- made from grapes
- contains mercury
- drink this wine with a knife and fork
- non kosher
- contains chicken
- contains BSE
- wine is also good garden fertiliser
- nine out of ten dog breeders recommend this wine
- best enjoyed by phone

CHAPTER 9
Putting wine down

Because what use is a wine to anyone unless it's at least twenty years old?

This is going to hurt me more than it hurts you, Tricky-Woo.
JAMES HERRIOTT

cellar alone is not enough. Anyone serious about wine not only needs a cellar under one's house, but also needs a cellarer and a cellaret. A cellarer, as my readers will know, is the rather nicer sounding English version of the German word *kellermeister* – that is, for new readers, a person (it best be a man) responsible for looking after the wine in one's cellar. A cellaret is a dining room sideboard in which one gets one's cellarer to place wines one's cellarer has been instructed to bring up from the cellar.

As this neat encapsulation of the process has readily pointed put, it is impossible to imagine life without all three of these vital steps – or 'protocols', as one is nowadays inclined to say.

'Putting wine down' is a term used to describe laying wine in, or secreting it away, or stowing fore and aft. Wine had its early popular enjoyment in the navy, and it is best not to forget such things.

Putting wine down also reminds many people of their favourite cat. The damn thing invariably gets itself lodged under the wheel of a passing vehicle and you have to go to all the trouble of dislodging it, only to subsequently discover it is still alive and needs treatment at the local veterinary hospital. Two days later the bill has run to more than the cost of three cases of Californian Wild Yeast Chardonnay – a wine of course that no vet, no matter how well trained, can ever hope to be able to put down.

Importantly, cellars need certain atmospheric conditions. Otherwise, one's wine may very well hold or even improve in the bottle. This is not and has never been the intention of cellaring. One should never believe any damn fool who suggests it is so. Cellaring is all about prestige and exclusivity. The best cellars are inherited along with the house. Buying someone else's cellar is like buying someone else's mother-in-law. And digging a cellar of your own is simply too repulsive an idea to discuss.

My above-ground cellar was bombed by the Germans in World War Two – damn those bloody Jerries!

Temperature

Wine is a living and breathing thing. What rot! It's dead. If we wanted to drink living, breathing beverages, we would all return to our youths and sup orange juice. Keep wine at a temperature that you find comfortable to live and eat in. If you are happy at this temperature, so ought your wine be.

Humidity

Humidity is a tropical disease that, in advanced cases, can bring on braided hair and tattoos – hardly the stuff for Fine Wine lovers. Avoid it at all costs. Zero humidity is perfect, particularly as it dries out corks and lets the wine breathe. To facilitate this process, keep your wine standing up. In recent times, the perverse trend of storing wine bottles on their sides has arisen, which I find a deviant, impure and sacrilegious act. It is true, of course, that wineries store their wine in this manner, but only to save space. I blame trendsetting lifestyle journalists for misapplying this industrial storage technique to home wine cellars.

Vibration

Those who suggest that vibration is bad for wine have obviously never drunk Madeira. The earth moves, and so doth wine.

Light

You will need strong light in your cellar to make sure you can see what is going on. I use candles – the burning wax reminds me of Blanc de Blancs Champagne, which reminds me to not buy any, as I don't particularly like it.

Sound

My great mate Sir Andrew Lloyd Webber has an enormous cellar full of the last century's best Beaujolais vintages. He – my apologies, Sir Andrew – has his cellar rigged up with a quadraphonic high-fidelity phonograph set on a continuous loop. This device plays his hit musicals over and over again at considerable volume. The wines seem to love it, for they are among the finest examples of aged Beaujolais I have ever tasted.

My great mate Andrew Lloyd Weber's cellar is protected by the ghost of the late Andre Simon. Apparently his spirit arrived in a bottle from a deceased estate.

Aspect

Underground is best for cellars, but for no other reason than tradition. Wine people are staunch traditionalists, and this is why cellars remain underground.

Keeping records

Your wine merchant is responsible for this.

WHEN IS IT READY?

Oh, if I only had a guinea for every time I had been asked that question. Wine, of course, is far too complex a miracle to ever possibly understand. I must naturally admit, of course, that I know more about it than most. Indeed, my great mate Stephen Hawking has been kind enough to say that I, Oberon Kant, am to wine what he, Stephen Hawking, is to cosmology. The truth of the matter is that wine is very rarely ever ready. More crucial to this age-old and deeply perplexing issue of vital human importance, however, is whether those people who drink wine are ever READY to drink it – let alone worthy. The barbarians are at the gates, I am appalled to have to say, and now wine is sold in supermarkets to the ape-like descendants of beer drinkers. Change and decay is all around I see…

CHAPTER 10

Wine and food

That old chestnut.

A meal without wine is like a day without sunshine.
KURT COBAIN

Arranging a marriage between one's food and one's wine is a chance for the epicure to truly shine in mixed company. Over thousands of years, man has perfected and developed set rules for food and wine-matching. It would be churlish of anyone to disregard these tenets – and foolish to apply them too casually. Of course, in recent times (I refer here only to this and the last century) some younger members of the food and wine medium have sought to vaingloriously abandon these strictures [refer Chapter 12: Wine and Health] – this amounts to a gastronomic *nolo episcopari*. My thoughts on this matter are well-documented, suffice to say that readers should be wary of this sort of ignorant and dangerous lifestyle journalism *sans* rules.

Food and wine rules, as I will presently and exhaustively expound, are not unlike one's times tables or corporal punishment. They ought to be learned and practised by rote. Anything less than a strict adherence to these laws will invariably result in moral decrepitude.

Fish

White wine is perfect with most fish.

There are two types of fish: pelagic and flying. Eat the former, beware the latter – especially at low altitude. My great mate and surfing champion Mark Occolupo was once impaled by a low-flying swordfish during a surfing trip to Ashmore Reef. It impaired his enjoyment of wine for at least six months. We can all learn from this. Fish is an excellent luncheon meat.

Cod: 10-year-old, second-growth Bordeaux from poorer years, such as 84.
Smoked Cod: as above, but only when one is suffering from a head-cold.
Salted Cod: avoid Portuguese table wines; try Moscato
Oysters: Krug.
Smoked Oysters: corked Krug.
Jellied Eel: Reichensteiner from one of the newer home counties wine-tourism facilities.

White meats

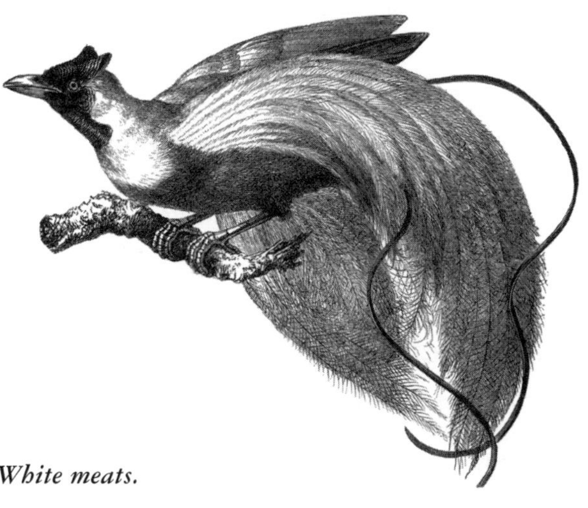

White meats.

I have it on very good authority that one must drink white wine with white meat. Personally I find it an inferior flesh without the iron-rich surge of blood that makes beef or venison an infinitely more sanguine dining experience.

Chicken: any suitably boring wine that will help you deal with this culinary papier-mâché. Australian red or white below five pounds Sterling, especially from UK supermarkets.

Pork: a luxury, deserving of the very best wine you can afford, such as Champagne and vodka.

Veal: I refuse to eat veal. The pleasure of the calf is in the hunt. When hunting and discussing Romantic poetry with my great mate Noel Edmonds at his country estate in Essex, I like to fill my hip flask with blushful Hippocrene, drawn straight from the fermenting vat.

Fava beans: chilled Chianti.

Starling: mineral water.

Shrimp (sometimes called prawns, particularly in my adopted homeland, Australia): Sonoma Chardonnay. Gallo, for example (she's a lovely gal, that Gina Gallo), at room temperature – the Chardonnay, not Gina (but then again ...).

Brains: animal-dependent but I unerringly opt for a subtle, delicate red wine like Barossa Shiraz – and a spoon.

Tripe: a thimbleful of Soave.

Heart, stuffed: Petrus, but on absolutely no account any other Merlot wine. At breakfast, dilute the Petrus with a drop of cold Ceylonese tea.

Beef

It is said that free-range beef has more flavour than lot-fed beef.

As my great-uncle Antoine de Brillat Savarin reminded me only the other day, beef is one of the most effective health tonics known to man – particularly when accompanied by the right wine.

Chateaubriand: This very much depends on the Michelin rating of the restaurant. I generally recommend Bordeaux (growths and vintages to match the quality of the eatery).
Bistecca alla Fiorentina: Chianti, but on no account a Super-Tuscan. Super-Tuscan indeed. Commercial Australian blends such as Grange can be suitable when dining at home.

CORNED BEEF: Claret; with caper sauce, pick recent vintages from odd years, such as 81, 83, 85 and so on; with Cornichons, choose even years such as 82, 86, 88 and so on; with sauce made from the boiled-down bones of a Thompson's gazelle, choose wines from leap years.
COLD CUTS: a case of any good quaffer; in hot weather: Cava.
GOOSE: Madeira, at exactly 25 years of age. Anything younger is unthinkably undrinkable; after that, it is too late.
DUCK: the true and the only, the ever willing yet somehow unwilling, the great wine of the world, Burgundy. (NB: I do not consider Peking Duck to be duck. Leading zoologists support this theory.)
COLD DUCK: Bollinger.

SAUSAGES

Sausages improve all wines. Indeed, in some countries sausages are a permitted wine additive. One version of the miracle at Cannae has Jesus turning water into sausages AND SAUSAGES INTO WINE. Martin Luther so fervently believed in this version of the trinity that he nailed 96 sausages to the door of the cathedral in Frankfurt. Thus was born one of the world's most popular sausage faiths.

WEISSWURST: the soft, yielding texture and delicate flavour of a good weisswurst call for a Hunter Valley Semillon of middle maturity – five years bottle age if the wine is from a warm vintage (seven if it is

Sausages help complete the well-rounded diet.

from a wet vintage). Ideally, the wine will be made in the traditional manner from 60-year-old vines in the Belford sub-region and served at ten degrees from standard tasting glasses.

Knackwurst: one of the few sausages I find better matched with a beer rather than a wine. You can't just open and fling down any old beer, though. It must be a malty pale ale from an old family-owned brewery in Suffolk, made using Star of Saffron Waldon hops and served in large pewter tankards.

Cevapcici: skinless, chilli-hot sausages like these call for a wide-open, spicy wine. I find almost anything from the Southern Rhone Valley works quite well, but nothing seems to match the grainy, almost coral-like texture of the sausages as well as a tobaccoey, macerated blood-plum-flavoured five-year-old Vacqueyras from a medium-sized co-operative. Hard to find perhaps, I'll grant you, but well worth the effort.

English pork: the very best match in the world for good old plump, pink, gristly English pork sausages is French artisan farmhouse cider from Brittany. But as I'm a realistic wine writer with my readers' interests uppermost in my mind, I've found you a highly acceptable alternative. Barry and Linda Gummer of the Scrumpy Hollow biodynamic orchard in the Atherton Tablelands in Queensland produce small quantities of vintage-dated scrumpy-style cider from their traditional French *Grobbette Noir* and *Maladie du Marche* apples. A deliciously murky, smokey, palate-drenching drop it is, too.

Chorizo: it is crucial to get a chorizo of the right age and spiciness, or you might as well kiss the whole food- and wine-matching thing goodbye. I use an eighteen-week-old sausage, bought direct from the manufacturer in Barcelona (0.5 per cent smoked, sweet paprika) and smuggled out of the country in the hollowed-out pages of an old copy of *Don Quixote*. I grill it gently and enjoy it – somewhat surprisingly, I suppose – with a light, herbaceous Chilean Cabernet from the early 1980s. The match intrigued me until it suddenly clicked: the sausage was redolent of smoked capsicum, while the wine was redolent of green capsicum! So simple and yet so brilliant.

Lup Cheong: my great mate and pork expert Barry Schitthe rustled up some of these classic, thin

Chinese sausages made from duck livers instead of the usual pork mince. The flavours (quite offally) and texture (dense, bloody) threw up an interesting wine challenge. Luckily, I had just the thing on hand: a big, bold, syrupy one-year-old Napa Valley Zinfandel. I suspect however, that almost any big red with more than sixteen per cent alcohol volume would do the trick – as long as you remember to cut the potentially fatal combination of lup cheong and ball-tearer by eating a small slither of cold cucumber with each mouthful of sausage and wine.
Andouillette: the ultimate challenge. This tumescent sack of intestines and tubes, with all its glistening slippery texture and unmistakable, uncompromising perfume of visceral reality is lovely with Rosé.

Game

Unlike veal, the pleasure of game is primarily in the eating. The fact that some people hunt these poor wild animals I find abhorrent.

Wild Boar: if hung in feather for three years and scraped from the carcass, boar is magnificent with Dry Sherry.
Quail (not hung, but stood upon): try aged Sauvignon Blanc from Hawkes Bay.
Rabbit: a wine with sufficient acidity to dissolve lead shot, such as Txacoli from the Basque country in northern Spain.
Hare: Californian jug wine and Womack and Womack purring deeply from a Dolby surround sound system.

Pheasant: Do not pluck! If I had a guinea for every time I have seen pheasant ruined by savage plucking I would be substantially wealthier than I already am. I am not afraid to say I am rich. Not only did I inherit money, but I made money as well. This is a lesson the younger generation would do well to learn. Sherry.

Wild Eel: Unfermented Chardonnay.

Kangaroo: classic regional foods should always be matched with classic regional wines. Try Ice Wine from Nova Scotia.

Field-picked mushrooms (from one's own field, or one's brother-in-law's): anything from what one's brother-in-law considers to be a rather grand cellar.

Salmon: a wine with sufficient acidity to dissolve lead shot, such as Txacoli from the Basque country in northern Spain.

Blow Fish: whatever is on the hospital's *carte du vins*.

EMPEROR PENGUIN: single vineyard Tokaji from the Royal Tokaji Wine Company. 'A regal wine for a regal bird', as my great mate Michael Caine used to say.
DOLPHIN: Madeira.
MINCE: once again, the true pleasure of mince is in the hunt. Unfortunately, mince is an endangered species in many parts of Britain, and the mincing season has been shortened to the first two weeks of summer. As a result, the market has been flooded with inferior grade farmed mince from Iran, Iraq and North Korea. This mince is only suitable to be served at the end of the meal. I have found that nothing goes with after-dinner mince.

CHEESE

As my great mate Mahatma Gandhi used to say, 'Man cannot live on Stilton alone'. How right he was, how right he was.

STILTON: Port.

VEGETABLES

If there is one thing that I never tire of railing against, it is our society's resolute ignorance of the importance of a healthy, balanced diet centred around the regular consumption of fresh, nutritious vegetables. Vegetables have high levels of essential vitamins, soluble fibre, minerals, anti-oxidant and aphrodisiac properties. The Ponds Institute has conclusively proved that a diet high in vegetables helps reverse the visible signs of ageing.

Roasted potatoes: 1963 Pomerol.
Boiled potatoes: 1964 Pomerol.
Steamed potatoes: 1965 Pomerol.
Chipped potatoes: 1966 Pomerol.
Fried potatoes: 1966 Pomerol.
Raw potatoes: 1967 Pomerol.
Smoked potatoes: 1968 Pomerol.
Sun-dried potatoes: 1999 White Zinfandel.
Preserved potatoes: 1970 Pomerol.
Salted potatoes: 1971 Pomerol.
Jugged potatoes: 1972 Pomerol.

Ethnic cuisines

The world is an amazing place. Whenever I venture into it I am constantly enthralled at the myriad of cultures and the way they fry food. It is truly a delight to taste the wonders of the world's kitchens and although not suitable to live upon, they make an enchanting departure from real food. Here is the fully comprehensive list of the cuisines of the world I collated for UNESCO on a wide-ranging fact-finding mission in 1973.

Chinese/Asian: wines high in additive 621.
Japanese: with its emphasis on dextrously presented and refined light dishes subtly exhibiting a complexity of delicate acidity and protein, Japanese cuisine is best accompanied by warm jugs of mulled Retsina.

Lebanese: despite years of war with neighbouring countries, the Lebanese have faithfully retained their ancient cooking and taxi driving traditions. Responsible taxi drivers only ever drink de-alcoholised Spumante.
Greek/Thai: Sauvignon Blanc.

Greek waiters wear national costume when serving skordalia.

Northern American: I suggest wines from Milwaukee. For more information I recommend any of the books by renowned wine-writing duo, Frank J. Laverne and Frank J. Shirley.
Indian: during my time as a colonel with the Third Punjabi Jabbers it was commonplace for the native

troops to place their members in a ceremonial bowl filled with the local rum on certain holy days. This practice was referred to as 'Rum Rogering', and was greatly enjoyed by the other ranks. While partaking of this on Regimental Day, I was unfortunate to come rather too close to the Tandoori oven. Thus today I am still known as 'Old Smokey' throughout the sub-continent.

Desserts

I consider myself somewhat lucky in that I never have to venture into the kitchen when it comes time to indulge in dessert. Every Friday, it has become a bit of a tradition chez Kant for passing international superstar cooks to drop in with a basket groaning with their latest sweet inventions. It is not unusual, to find Martha Stewart, Elizabeth David, Delia Smith, Nigella Lawson, Marcella Hazan, Claudia Roden, J. K. Rowling and Richard Olney jostling for space at my titanium bench-tops – the kitchen resounding with their girlish laughter as they whisper culinary sweet

Aaah… Elizabeth David as I remember her.

nothings into each other's ears. All I need do is recline in my favourite rather worn but terrifically comfortable armchair as my staff bring me decadent nibbles of this and exquisite tastes of that. Towards the end of the evening, my great-aunt Isabella Beeton often props herself up on her walking frame next to the stove and makes cleansing junket for us all. Ah, happy days.

Black Forest gateau: 1982 Leoville-Barton, en magnum.
Trifle: Manzanilla Pasada Sherry (a half-bottle per man).
Croquenbuche: Barrel-fermented botrytised Viognier.
Crème caramel: any 1970s vintage of Australia's Wolf Blass Black Label.
Crème brûlée: 10-year-old New World Chardonnay, preferably cellared in the trunk on one's old Morris Minor Runabout.
Crepe suzette: de-alcoholised Spumante.
Pudding: Horlicks.

Useful numbers

CHAPTER II

What, when and why to drink

Wines to suit every occasion.

If the man who sits beneath the shade of his own vines, his family by his side, a glass of his own wine clasped in his hand, still finds himself unhappy, he should remarry.
JAMES BUSBY, 1856

s one of my former students, Sam Beckett, used to say, life is an unremitting series of meaningless coincidences that propel us towards the grave, our pathetic attempts to resist the inevitable only serving to underline what futile and ineffectual head lice we are, crawling eternally on the craggy scalp of a bleak existence – unless one has a glass of Claret or Madeira in hand, in which case life can be rather jolly.

Wine indubitably enhances every occasion. Without wine, life is not worth living. Here is a selection of real-life situations that you may find yourself in. Try them with wine. I guarantee you will not be disappointed.

Après petit déjeuner

As my great mate Larry Hagman called that time in the morning between breakfast and elevenses, *Après petit déjeuner* is a few hours when Champagne is no longer a wine but a light classical background score to the everyday theatre of life.

Morning tea

Tea, scones, jam and neutral grape spirit – a time-honoured tradition.

Afternoon tea

Tea, scones, jam and neutral grape spirit will always strengthen one's appetite.

Cocktail hour

Enjoy Madeira. (Under no circumstances should you ever drink cocktails. They are a pathetic attempt to sell rotten fruit or rancid dairy products fortified with chemically made spirits. They are, in a word, morally affronting.)

Vespers

When the bells start ringing I pour a glass of Port made by my great mate Brother John May, Jesuit winemaker at Sevenhill in South Australia's Clare Valley.

Sundown

Madeira, of course.

When royalty drops in

I always had a bottle of Gilbey's handy, just in case Margaret dropped by. I kept a bottle in my filing cabinet and a carton of Benson & Hedges in the non-fiction section of the library for those occasional sojourns.

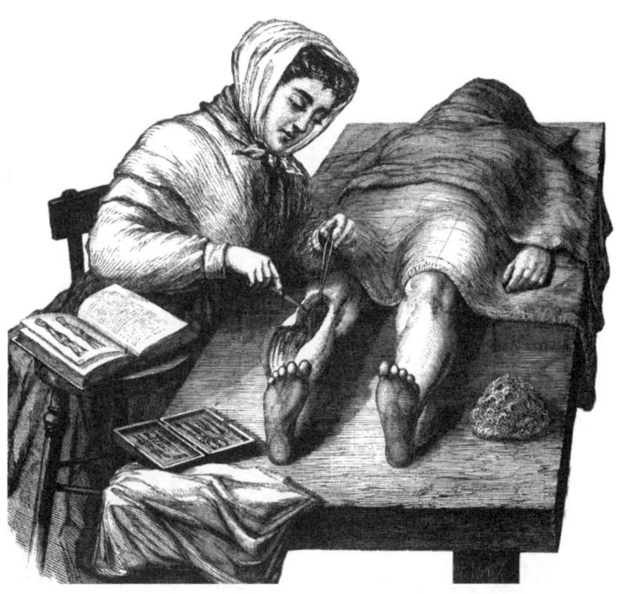

Surgical operations

A friend of mine at St Bart's in London always took a neat nip of Jaegermeister before every procedure. He was later struck off after being spuriously accused of touching a nurse. English brain surgery wasn't the same without him. He still practices in South Africa where he performs the odd lobotomy fortified by a coffee mug of this great Teutonic hunting beverage.

Before trying on shoes

It's not so much about what to drink in this situation as what *not* to drink. Avoid fortified wines several days before buying a new pair of shoes. This will stop any gouty swelling and allow you to procure a pair of shoes that are your correct size. (I am in the unfortunate position of having one foot a full size-and-a-half larger than the other.) I find shoe shopping a laborious and time-consuming process, so when I need new footwear I offer a glass of decent Bonnezeaux, which I have secreted in my overcoat pocket, to the poor shop assistant to help him find a pair of odd shoes in their remnant collection.

Apres ski

Invigorating, cold and lofty, the Swiss Alps always remind me of my grandmother's attic – where I'd curl up as a very young man, my uncle's collection of postcards in one hand and a jug of mulled wine in the other.

Waiting on hold

Whenever I have a quick chat to department stores or utility providers about the inevitably appalling service or goods they provide, I invariably find myself placed on hold in a telephone queue. After twenty minutes or so, my spirits begin to lag. My good mate Ralph Nader once told me he sips on a can of Bud Lite to perk him up. I, on the other hand, find that a good phone stoush runs better after a half-bottle or so of third-growth St Estephe.

Opera

Drinking at La Scala was banned after a friend of the Duke of Urbino fell from the balcony and was impaled on the helmet spike of a large Valkyrie. Opera houses around the world soon followed suit with the ban. A friend of mine, very close to Buckingham Palace, manages to endure the likes of Il *Travatore* and *Tristan and Isolde* by filling her opera glasses with Dry Sherry. A tube runs from the space between the lenses to her mouth. Every time she raises her glasses to enjoy another joyous mouthful of Palo Cortado, anyone watching would simply think she is admiring the tenor.

Theatre

Never order interval drinks before a play. Horrendous oxidisation occurs in those draughty theatres. It is therefore essential to have a good education and know the texts of every play verbatim. Make your excuses two lines before the end of the first act, wander up to the bar and avoid the hoi polloi.

Hosting a current affairs show

A wine glass of chilled blended scotch (never single malt whisky) by your side gets one through the toughest of interviews.

'Choose your wine before your midwife,' my mother always said. Here she is photographed soon after giving birth to me. Note her happiness.

Birth

My mother always had a breathtakingly flinty Meursault after every one of her seven arduous births. I remember having family meals as a young adult with my siblings when mother, God bless her, would recount every detail of our entrance into this world with long soliloquies describing not the pain she endured, but praising the quality of the wine she drank as the midwife swaddled us in cotton blankets. She was later institutional in organising a charity fund to provide sommeliers in antenatal clinics around the globe.

Picnics

A Shiraz high in formic acid is my drink of choice on such occasions. The smell of crushed ants will disguise the smell of crushed ants.

Garden-pest control

Small saucers of beer placed around the garden are easy to drink from while kneeling to remove snails.

Book launches

A fine brandy, a shooting stick and a book from one's own library. These things can go on for hours.

An Irish wake

Every facet of these dear Celtic people's lives is lubricated by a dark, thick, bitter liquid that is better described as a foodstuff than as a drink. Irish stout, I'm afraid, is far too viscous and hearty – it is a brewed malt soup, not a beverage. Nonetheless, when Irish are born, the event is celebrated with pints of Guinness; when they are married they celebrate with Guinness; when they purchase postage stamps of a particular denomination they nip down to Seamus O'Hannarahan's for a night on the Guinness. It is, I believe, part of their constitution to mark every single daily occurrence with several gallons of stout. In fact, even the most devout Muslim airlines allow Guinness to be consumed while flying in Irish airspace out of respect for the local religion. It comes as no surprise, dear reader, to find that the black stuff is poured as soon as a compatriot ceases to be. Some local priests have a large wolfhound follow them to perform the last rites – a cask of Guinness secured around its neck. So when attending the all too frequent funerals of my many good writer chums, I'm far too sensitive to appear to be drinking anything other than Guinness. I do, however, despise the stuff, so I pour a bottle of young Mogador into a pint glass and cover the top with dairy cream. I maintain the appearance of adhering to eons of tradition while softening the harsh tannins with a coating of fresh butterfat.

Before a libel case

I still can't believe it is a crime to speak one's own mind. All too often I find myself dressed to the nines, beak at my side, in front of a judge defending what I have written about the appalling practices of New World winemakers. Before any appearance I sniff, swirl and listen at/around/to their product, then, with the taste of silver nitrate on my lips, I proceed to the courtroom and deliver an outstanding defensive oratory. Naturally the case is settled out of court with massive damages awarded in my favour.

Riding

Controlling a large powerful beast on a long ride requires special consideration. I recommend a high-quality Tokaji, for nothing is too good for one's horse.

The barber

High-alcohol old vine Zinfandel dabbed on the back of the neck quickly cauterises any bleeding. My barber

Emilio is nearly 80 and totally blind, but he still cuts hair beautifully through his heightened sense of touch and smell.

Weddings

Unless they are royal occasions I have always refused wedding invitations, including several of my own. The food is poor, the wine appalling and the company loathsome. If one does not have the moral fortitude to escape attending these banal displays of public hypocrisy, or if one is the best man – a truly worthy and honourable position – then purchase a specially constructed top hat, inside which bottles of the wine of your choice can be carefully secreted. As one's cranium emits a large amount of heat, I suggest you choose a wine best served at or near blood temperature, such as Madeira.

Holed up in grim military situations

This is the only time I would ever recommend dark rum, apart from veterinary emergencies.

Fashion parades

My God! Blow hard enough on a catwalk model and you'd flense the flesh from the poor creature's bones. Living on a constant diet of cocaine, cigarettes and camera flash has turned once beautiful women into human whippets. I implore you, dear reader, whenever you attend one of these cruel events, force-feed these girls as much fibre and vitamin-enriched vintage Port as they can stomach. Port? Yes Port.

When in doubt

Madeira, naturally.

Emergency contacts

CHAPTER 12

Wine and health

There is an awful lot of talk about wine and health these days.

Concentrate, concentrate. Concentrate on the spoon.
URI GELLER

I became interested in wine when I was born, as my readers well know, but my interest in wine and health only arose during my university days while studying for a triple degree in surgery, constitutional law and philology. Those were the days – when wine was ours and wine was enjoyed by people like us. The past is a different country, however (as I once said to an old literary mate of mine), and they do things differently there.

Yet I digress. Moderation is the only curse of the post-modern age, or period, as I think it ought to be properly labelled. Wine is healthful; moderation is the new plague.

At a recent Alcohol and Wine in Health and Disease Conference held in San Francisco, I delivered a short lecture on the very topic of the evils of moderation. During the course of my multimedia presentation, I single-handedly consumed a glass of Fino Sherry, a half-bottle of Bienvenues-Batard-Montrachet, a magnum of 89 Richebourg (as I was not eating, I thought Burgundy best, and I was right), and a half-bottle of LBVP, the name of which, for some reason, has temporarily escaped me.

Such moderation seriously affected the power of the speech. It was good, let there be no doubt, but the lecture could have been better. How? This is clearly a rhetorical question employed solely for the sake of literary variation because I know how.

Therefore, and in as much the name of science as anything else, I delivered the very same lecture the following morning, to the same delegates, but with a more suitable range of refreshments.

Two martiniis were followed by a bottle of 85 Bollinger Rosé; then I played with two vintages of Klusserath from the Mittel-Mosel (the 76 and the 83, incidentally); as a haunch of aged Brown Bear was served, I drank an imperial of 59 La Mission-Haut-Brion, without decanting; and I ended my lecture anecdotally, while musing over a slightly ullaged bottle of 1791 Sandeman Madeira. Two hours became seven; my presentation was dynamic, compelling, entertaining and moving. Indeed, more than one of the delegates was so profoundly affected by my searing insights coupled with my unbridled orotund deliverance that they were moved to tears.

I therefore conclude – nay, prove – that in matters vinous, moderation maketh man weak! Drinking deeply from the horn aplenty, with purple-stained mouth, doth turn boys into men and men into heroes.

Grape-skin polyphenols may be powerful antioxidants and these may in turn prevent low density lipoproteins from coating artery walls while simultaneously stimulating nitrous oxide formation, thus increasing blood flow and helping to decrease the risk of ischaemic strokes, but why bother recounting these

When women stray too far from the Pimms.

old wives tales when one can demonstrate from one's own evidence and experience the positive effects of proper wine consumption?

As a guide, I recommend people drink at least a bottle of wine a day – white and red. They should also use fortified wines and pre-luncheon spirits at their own discretion. Womenfolk, is it clear enough, should not drink as much as other people; but for the sake of sociability may use Pimms as a stop-gap while the chaps continue on with the wine. A recent and perverse phenomenon, known as the Alcohol-Free Day, strikes me as being as destructive to man's culture as the abandonment of the Latin liturgy.

Wines to drink when you are unwell

Since the beginning of time, during Hippocrates' 45-year reign as president of the Athenian Medical Association, various wine styles have been used to combat life's unpleasantnesses. Here are some examples still in common use across the western world.

Head-colds: young Riesling, taken day and night.
Pox: douse the concerned areas with highly acidic Blanc de Blancs Champagne and inhale athletically.
Homosexuality: no cure; addiction to bad New World Pinot Noir is a telltale symptom, however.
Obesity: drink until you throw up. Spots of blood in one's vomit are a very healthy sign.

Drunkenness: a congenital disease; wine connoisseurs do not suffer from it, however.
Shark/tiger/bear bite: sluice wound with Gevrey-Chambertin; carry on.
Shooting accidents: brandy or grappa at a pinch. Drink it all down in one go. Shooting anyone (even family) can be a traumatic experience, so best be on the safe side.
Pregnancy: drink Claret and hope she goes away.

Wines to cure common ailments

Atheism: Chateuneuf du Pape, while kneeling.
Lilly-livered, wet liberalism: brandy and soda consumed on the hour, every hour, until symptoms disappear.
Tolerance: see above.
The humours: German Riesling.
Ugliness: a temporary condition in others progressively cured by the continued ingestion of any wine under controlled, dimly-lit conditions.
Gardening, demonic possession, Communism: all variants of the common cold. Drop two aspirin into a glass of Chablis. Rest.

This page to be left blank

Epilogue

What I shall be drinking this year.

Two things fill the mind with ever increasing wonder and awe – the starry heavens above me and the Madeira within me.
Critique of Pure Wines, IMMANUEL KANT

Many people – especially those of the younger variety – ask me what I, in an ideal world, would like to drink. As with most questions muddlingly posed by people born after the war, one needs to do a fair bit of spade work on the question itself before any kind of answer can be properly attempted.

To begin with, there is no 'ideal' about it. I drink very much in the 'real world', or 'world', as our habitat was once rather neatly described. And I drink every day – with the odd (very rare) exception, such as when I am meditating with my great mate Deepak Chowder.

I do not consider myself in any way privileged by my circumstances and enormous cellar and many and varied contacts with great friends who happen to either make, distribute, or promote the world's greatest and rarest and most expensive and sought-after wines. It is merely my job. Yes, my job. I am not too proud to work, which is a valuable lesson many young people might care to learn.

So this year I will be drinking the following wines. I

present them in rough chronological order, starting at dawn, through to breakfast, morning tea, luncheon, then lunch, afternoon tea, and so on.

Upon rising

Pink gin made with Land's End Gin: from my great mate and distant relative Rodney Camelworthy-Cant, the Djin of Gin, whose arm of the family has been hand-crafting this superb gin for over 400 years. They use no juniper whatsoever in their secret list of botanicals and flavourings, instead preferring to use Patak's Mango Chutney. Rodders lost an arm in Korea, so his results are even more outstanding than you might imagine.

Breakfast

Lambrusco: from Podiola-Cant, a distant cousin who is kind enough to air freight a pallet of this breakfast wine to me every spring.

Morning tea

Sherry: this is when the day really starts to take shape, and I am once again capable of conducting simple tasks such as signing my own name, finding the front door, and passing stools. What a wonderful drink sherry is. One tends to rarely drink more than a bottle – unless one is entertaining.

Luncheon

A range of Clarets from Bordeaux, such as La Haut-Terse Millieu, Canon Potet-Maillard Du, or Chateau Kant-Peynaud-Johnson, a small estate on the east-north-east bank of which I am lucky enough to be part owner.

At Lunch

A range of Burgundy wines – whites then reds.

Afternoon tea

This is the time of day when I tend to drink late-bottled Vintage Port or, in the warmer weather, White Port. The best comes from Quinta Nova Cant-Cockburn-Croft, founded by one of my ancestors and two of his school chums back in 1796 – amazingly while they were all still at Eton.

In that awkward hour between afternoon tea and dinner

This is the time for one to partake of a restorative – brandy and soda is perfect. Not too much ice, mind. Less on the soda but go long on the brandy – otherwise the medicine will not take proper effect. This is when the day really starts to take shape, and I am once again capable of conducting simple tasks such as signing my own name, finding the front door, and passing stools. What a wonderful drink sherry is.

Upon arriving at dinner

Champagne (vintage only). One of the masculine houses – such as Bollinger – and preferably with considerable bottle-age. Of late, I have been particularly enjoying the 1927, in hand-blown magnums. It really is a waste of time to bother with anything else.

Dinner

Strangely, I am often so swept up in the food, beauty, sparkling conversation and rapier-like wit of my hostess, that I find myself unable to recall the great wines I have chosen to accompany the repast.

After Dinner

And then, finally, when one is at last alone with one's thoughts in the comfort of one's favourite armchair, and as dawn breaks over the mighty Murray River – and as a new dawn of sorts is breaking for wine-lovers everywhere – one can find solace in a glass or two of fine Madeira.

Glossary

All of wine's myriad words, phrases and lexicons explained, demystified and neatly tied up with string.

Man acts as though he were the shaper and master of language, while in fact language remains the master of man. Oops!
BRITNEY SPEARS

Language is a wonderful servant but a costly mistress. Every year, thousands of new words enter our ever-expanding vocabulary. Ignore them all; use only the tried-and-tested words and terms listed here. They will never fail you.

GRAPE GROWING TERMS

PETIOLE: pathetic.
REGULATED DEFICIT IRRIGATION: a bowel spasm experienced by a vigneron when noticing his grapes are petiole.
SHRINKAGE: a problem affecting wine regions that experience large diurnal shifts. Vineyards in such areas can often shrink at night, leaving much of your crop inside your neighbouring vigneron's chateau the next morning.
APPLE MOTH, LIGHT BROWN: an airborne insect that prefers to travel by land; can ruin apple crops, therefore seriously affecting cool climate Chardonnay quality.

Terroir: a French nonsense word used by New World wine experts who know nothing about real viticulture.
Burning off: an Australian technique designed to limit extreme vigour in vines.
Hen and chicken: a philosophical conundrum, as in 'which came first?'
Millerandage: a French term; see above.
Stamen: (biblical) a man's seed.
Ferret: French; a vineyard worker's hat.
Pole: geographical term indicating your position in relationship to either the north or south poles. Very useful for establishing potential Heat Degree Days, as in: 'we are only two or three poles away from a perfect vintage'.
Tanunda: South African chant, as in: 'Tanunda. Tanunda-a-ah. She's got diamonds on the soles of her shoes.'
Tequila: Mexican insecticide.
Blenheim: a muffled sneeze.

Winemaking terms

Einzefellungen: archaic Bavarian term for the process of live egg-white fining, where a whole chicken (eggus interruptus) is submerged in a barrel.
Elbow: anatomical term; can become roughened and the skin irreparably damaged in wineries with too many wooden surfaces.
Knackers: anatomical term; can become roughened and the skin irreparably damaged in wineries with

too many wooden surfaces.
PIGEAGE: old pigeons, good for shooting yet stringy to eat.
ROASTING THE GUINEA FOWL: (Old English) to bring in the first grapes of the winter.
GRAN RESERVA: a popular Spanish banking house.
DIPOLO ELECTRICO: the use, by some Italians, of high-voltage electricity to kill yeast when sulphur is scarce.
HARD STITCH: to add tannin to fermenting wine by hand, as opposed to by the bucket-load.
THE BEATLES: a recent, popular musical ensemble.
LSD: Limited Slip Differential.
BIGGLES: my favourite wine hero.
BARBARA CARTLAND: an aunt and, although it is oft forgot, the first female wine columnist (The Telegraph).
CORK: Irish county famous for seafood and banshees.
ORGANIC WINE: wine for bearded anti-nuclear demonstrators. Morally corrupt.
WINEMAKER: popular face of a wine company often hired from casting agencies. Increasingly a part played by women.
BRAND MANAGER: a winemaker.
MARKETING MANAGER: the person with the credit card.
WINE SHOW: public display critical to the ongoing success of the wine industry and a jolly good chance to catch up with a few mates. The only way to accurately taste 1000 wines in a day.
UNIVERSITY: where I met Evelyn Waugh.
FLEUR: a lovely young girl in publicity.

Lees: yeast faeces. Australians dye it with shoe polish and put it on toast.
Spurty: Scottish term of endearment.

Tasting terms

Ethical: the way wine used to taste, before supermarkets came along and spoiled it all.
Honest wine: wine you can trust. Wine that you can send out with your daughter, safe in the knowledge that she'll be home by ten, fully operational.
Duty: the moral tax we must pay in some form or another to society's greater gain.
Obligation: reaching the end of the bottle once it has been opened.
Family: people who fail to grasp the concept of obligation.
Society: lax.
Financial responsibility: buying wine is financially responsible. Joining a gym is clearly not.
Bugger: any wine that reminds one of one's university career.
Muller Thurgau: archaic Bavarian term for 'interesting'.
Decoupage: how much wine a women can hold in her cleavage, measured in half-pints.
Disgorge: (Creole) to remove wine from a woman's cleavage.
Scraping the bottom of the barrel: a Fine to Very Fine Wine, complete with acceptable traces of dekkara.

Barding: to make a wine sing [see Chapter 2: How to Taste Wine Properly].
Squeal like a pig: a typical flavour profile of any young Riesling insufficiently corrected with sugar.
Carrion twang: similar to 'scraping the bottom of the barrel' but entirely different; best used to describe any wine made in the New World by someone with a Latin surname.
Oeil-de-perdrix: a delicacy.
Kladderadatsch: a delicacy.
Extra mild: wine descriptor ideally suited to New World Chardonnay.
Bordeaux: Claret.
Burgundy: Burgundy.
Madeira: wine in its purest form.
Chardonnay: not Madeira.
Beer: form of sparkling wine.
Vodka: very austere Riesling.

Wine buying terms

Port: a light luncheon wine for summer.
Cork taint: a myth promulgated by aluminium corporations.
Jacobs Creek: English nudist colony.
Blue Nun: enigmatic wine named after Sister Willhelmina Gotha and the only white wine I've ever been able to drink with rare beef.
Mateus: French abstract painter. Not my cup of tea. I believe, towards the end of what he laughingly called his career, he frequently painted with his penis.
Mise en Bouteille: French for 'buyer-beware'.

Also, staggeringly-beautiful modern opera by my great chum, Sir Andrew Lloyd Webber. He once suggested that much of the libretto was inspired by one Oberon Kant. He is too kind.
Special: would you buy a 'special' dog from a pet shop? I think not.
Discounted: morally bankrupt.
End of stock/end of lease/end of line: not sure, no, don't help me, I've got it, tip of the tongue ... no, no, it's gone.
Good wine: I loathe mediocrity.
Bargain: unethical, see below.
Summer quaffer: chilled Port.
Summer quaffers: San Francisco, 1973, hand in hand, me, Armistead and a lovely young blonde boy from Idaho ...

Other useful terms

Back label: old English phrase as used in *Henry VI Part III*. Falstaff to Prince Hal: 'Be gone you foul liquid fool / Back, label! Back!'
Mogadon: a Spanish wine.
Cerapax: a character from *Ulysses.*
Ulysses: a wine bar in Baggot Street near St Stephen's Green.
Wine lake: mythical place.
Wine conference: mythical place.
Wine knowledge: (Old Anglo Saxon) a myth.
Wine journalism: most important form of literature known to man.
Wine flagon: a small drinking vessel.

Wine cask: breathing apparatus.
Product life cycle: how many times a bottle of Lambrusco will repeat on you at 1 a.m. while relaxing in a lap-dancing bar.
Lap-dancing bar: a Fine Wine establishment.
Maître d: a Frenchman.
Garcon: Yves Montand film.
Sommelier: a barman.
Pommelier: potato expert. A profession far too under-appreciated, I'm sorry to say.
Cheese: stilton.
Tea: a drop with jam and bread.
Ullage: a town in Northern Ireland and centre of the Troubles.
Stelvin: an aluminium Texan hat.
Salubrity: the state of one's health after drinking a bottle of wine for luncheon.
Luncheon: 1) a light meal taken before lunch at about midday; 2) a useful term for describing the light, playful qualities of wines from great estates during bad vintages.

Terms to avoid at all costs

Some of these oeno-neologisms have captured the retarded imaginations of the new wine journalists (and I use the term 'journalist' rather loosely), with their unkempt hair and side burns, their open-neck shirts and garishly coloured portable computers. These terms have no place in the language of wine; the use of such words only helps to further destroy the moral fabric of our society.

PLUMMY:
FRUITY:
FUNKY:
SEXY:
RAUNCHY:
RACY:
YUMMY:
CRUNCHY:

Definitions? No. These terms have no definitions as they are used (or abhorrently misused) by new wine journalists with no real meaning in mind. Their only function is one of infantile linguistic rhythm; they serve a loose and very primitive poetic purpose designed to disguise the fact that the new wine journalist knows nothing about wine at all. Onomatopoeia is thus sullied and all wine is henceforth reduced to barbarism. 'How good does it make ya feel?' they ask, as if such selfishness answers the very question of life itself. Such nausea makes me nauseous. I shall now take a half glass of Madeira and lie down [see Chapter 12: Wine and Health].

Appendix

Vintage charts

Because wine varies from year to year in each of the world's wine regions – that, indeed, is its unending majesty, mystery and magic – I enclose here for my readers' benefit a comprehensive list of the past century's great vintages in all of those regions, using my own clear system of cleverly calibrated quality ratings, ingeniously cross-referenced to the climatic data and census information as it relates to the local population and property values in the capital cities and towns of the districts. I dare say you will find these charts enormously helpful.

Madeira

226 AUSTRALIAN HOME COOKERY

MADEIRA CAKE

INGREDIENTS

5 oz. sugar
4 oz. butter
4 oz. S.R. flour
3 eggs
4 oz. plain flour
4 tablespoons milk
Grated rind 1 lemon

Method.—Beat butter and sugar to a cream. Add the eggs, well beaten, blend well. Sift the two flours together, and add by degrees, beating well each time. Add the grated lemon, then the milk slowly. Give a final beat. Turn into a round, deep tin, previously greased, and put into a moderately-hot oven for 10 minutes. Lower the temperature without opening the oven door, and cook in a moderate oven from 30 to 45 minutes.

Burgundy

PHONETIC TRANSCRIPTION OF FRENCH

Vowels	
i	il, vie, lyre
e	blé, jouer
ɛ	lait, jouet, merci
a	plat, patte
ɑ	bas, pâte
ɔ	mort, donner
o	mot, dôme, eau, gauche
u	genou, roue
y	rue, vêtu
ø	peu, deux
œ	peur, meuble
ə	le, premier
ɛ̃	matin, plein
ɑ̃	sans, vent
ɔ̃	bon, ombre
œ̃	lundi, brun

Semi-consonants	
j	yeux, paille, pied
w	oui, nouer
ɥ	huile, lui

Consonants	
p	père, soupe
t	terre, vite
k	cou, qui, sac, képi
b	bon, robe
d	dans, aide
g	gare, bague
f	feu, neuf, photo
s	sale, celui, ça, dessous, tasse, nation
ʃ	chat, tache
v	vous, rêve
z	zéro, maison, rose
ʒ	je, gilet, geôle
l	lent, sol
ʀ	rue, venir
m	main, femme
n	nous, tonne, animal
ɲ	agneau, vigne
h	hop ! (exclamative)
'	haricot (no liaison)
ŋ	words borrowed from English: camping
x	words borrowed from Spanish or Arabic: jota

California

TOP 10 ★

HIGHEST-EARNING "BEST PICTURE" OSCAR WINNERS

	FILM	YEAR
1	*Titanic*	1997
2	*Forrest Gump*	1994
3	*Dances With Wolves*	1990
4	*Rain Man*	1988
5	*Schindler's List*	1993
6	*Shakespeare in Love*	1999
7	*The English Patient*	1996
8	*American Beauty*	1999
9	*Braveheart*	1995
10	*Gone With the Wind*	1939

Warragul dogs

1. Jinks Catering 7.12

$1000 Maiden Heat (1) 424 Metres

1-	23238	Won't Back Down, 5.0	NBT
2-	434	Konrad Bale, 6.0	FS
3-	27834	Smurf's Velocity, 9.0	NBT
4-	3	White Thunder, 5.0	FS
5-	3	Ahoy There, 9.0	NBT
6-	54337	Brad's Gem, 8.0	NBT
7-	72334	Inner Fire, 9.0	NBT
8-	13	Jetmaster, 3.0	FS
		Reserves	
9-	185	Stacey, 4.5	NBT
10-	27	Auto Zoom, 11.0	FS

Race 1 Selections 2-6-5-9

2. Carlton Draught 7.35

$1000 Maiden Heat (2) 424 Metres

1-	F2744	Drought Breaker, 9.0	NBT
2-	25	Broad Thought, 8.0	FS
3-	42425	No Addition, 4.0	NBT
4-	8737	Shigga Vale, 13.0	NBT
5-	28	Finn's Penny, 5.0	FS
6-	21	Brooklyn Rain, 3.0	FS
7-	424	Roman Candle, 4.5	FS
8-	2542	Leita, 8.0	NBT
		Reserves	
9-	6	Peerless Tess, 9.0	FS
10-	7	Pete's Gem, 11.0	NBT

6. Drouin Motors 8.54

$1285 Grade 4 424 Metres

1-	23341	Private Idaho, 4.0	24.44
2-	51773	Senor Valdez, 13.0	24.54
3-	71177	Evelyn Bale, 3.5	24.73
4-	F7676	Dianna Who, 13.0	24.28
5-	34127	Jocka, 4.5	24.42
6-	41367	Moulin Rouge, 8.0	24.45
7-	42446	Trios Pinari, 9.0	24.34
8-	86313	Jonanthy, 5.0	24.28
		Reserves	
9-	86686	Maxine Bale, 16.0	24.64
10-	38733	Ours It Is, 8.0	24.72

Race 6 Selections 8-1-5-6

7. Meadow Park Stud 9.12

$1215 Grade 5 424 Metres

1-	87727	Gert The Flirt, 13.0	24.28
2-	73612	Cheng Su Flyer, 2.75	NBT
3-	44525	Schwatta, 6.0	24.30
4-	56532	Jimbo, 8.0	NBT
5-	27215	Redhot Gal, 9.0	24.29
6-	32434	Solo Waters, 11.0	24.34
7-	57134	Southern Justice, 5.5	24.27
8-	45533	Meadow Magic, 5.0	24.57
		Reserves	
9-	38543	Nargin Lass, 11.0	NBT
10-	42586	Shy Shiraz, 11.0	NBT

Race 7 Selections 2-3-7-8

Acknowledgements

I could never, ever have contemplated writing this comprehensive book without the help of my closest and dearest mates including (but not limited to):

Larry Hagman; Barbara Walters; Bill Gates; Aaron Spelling; Andre Agassi; Barbra Streisand; David Hasselhof; Donald Trump; Gore Vidal; Noam Chomsky; Ricardo Montalban; Ted Turner & Jane Fonda; the Aga Khan; my Aga; Princess Fergie, the Duchess of Kent; Princess Stephanie of Monaco; Princess Fiona of Shrek; Yasser Arafat; Ariel Sharon; Charlton Heston; Roger Moore; David Copperfield; Nicki Lauda; Shirley Maclaine; Greg Norman; Daryl Somers; Tom Cruise & Nicole Kidman; HRH Prince Charles; Oprah Winfrey; Michael Parkinson; Richie Benaud; Jerry Springer; Billy Joel; Billy Jean King; Puffing Billy; Puff 'n' Stuff; Elton John & George Michael; Marcel Marceau; Burt Bacharach; Hugh Johnson; Stuart Gregor; Jancis Robinson; Robert Parker Snr; Ray Parker Jr; Robert Parker Jnr; Rupert Murdoch Snr; E. & J. Gallo; Tommy Suharto; Robert Mugabe; General Augusto Pinochet; Sting; Werner Klemperer; Stephen Hawking; Milan Kundera; David Irving; Christo; Christie's; Willie Schroeder; Wolfgang Puck; Mohamed Al Fayed; Mother Theresa; Princess Diana; Gidget; Yoko Ono; Hillary Rodham Clinton.

I would also like to take this opportunity to thank my staff at the groundbreaking food and wine web portal www.Spittoon.com.au Daisy Ireland, Barry Schitthe, Morbius, Dr Beaker Halifax, Martin Vagabond, Donna Hey! and Bere-Bere.

And a special thanks to Barry Humphries.

And my personal assistant, Mrs Jennifer Mousetrap.

And the dear, dear, lovely ladies – too many to mention by name – at my publishing house, Hardie Grant.

Without the generous assistance of the following companies, the publication of this book would have been entirely possible: Microsoft, Shell, Union Carbide, Accor Asia Pacific, Microsoft, Monsanto, Ciba Geigy, the Ponds Institute and Microsoft.

And my great mate Sir Les Patterson – a real wine man.

And finally, the genie that resides in every bottle.

And to all those enthusiasts with whom I have enjoyed some of the great food and wine of the world.